Sadlier PHONICS

LEVEL B

Jane M. Carr   Joanne M. McCarty

Patricia Scanlon   Anne F. Windle

Program Consultants

Grace R. Cavanagh, Ed.D.
Principal, P.S. 176
Board of Education
New York, New York

Vilma M. Vega, Ed.D.
Elementary Curriculum Supervisor
Hillsborough County Public Schools
Tampa, Florida

Patricia N. Grant
Director, Early Childhood Program
Sacred Heart School, Vailsburg
Newark, New Jersey

Donna A. Shadle
Kindergarten Specialist
St. Paul Elementary School
North Canton, Ohio

Eleanor M. Vargas
Resource Specialist Teacher
Los Angeles Unified School District
Los Angeles, California

Deborah A. Scigliano
First Grade Teacher
Assumption School
Pittsburgh, Pennsylvania

Sadlier-Oxford
A Division of William H. Sadlier, Inc.
New York, New York 10005–1002

Advisors

Stephanie Hart Brazell
Kindergarten/First Grade Teacher
Thousand Oaks, California

Sr. Paul Mary Janssens, O.P.
Principal
Aurora, Illinois

Sue Pecci
First Grade Teacher
Winter Springs, Florida

Debra L. Bates
Kindergarten/First Grade Teacher
Cleveland, Ohio

Damaris Hernandez-Reda
Assistant Principal
New York, New York

Sr. Dawn Gear, G.N.S.H.
Principal
Lilburn, Georgia

Mary L. Brown
Kindergarten/First Grade
Multi-Age Teacher
Chillicothe, Ohio

Theresa A. Kenney-Martinez
First Grade Teacher
Pomona, California

Anita Shevette
Kindergarten Teacher
Pomona, California

Sr. Paulette Marie Gregoire,
R.J.M.
Principal
Fall River, Massachusetts

Noelle Deinken
Kindergarten Teacher
Thousand Oaks, California

Mary Lee Gedwill
Second Grade Teacher
North Olmstead, Ohio

Angela L. Stankiewicz
Principal
New Bedford, Massachusetts

JoAnne Nardone, Ed.D.
Program Review Specialist
New York, New York

Sr. Francis Helen Murphy, I.H.M.
Editorial Advisor
Immaculata, Pennsylvania

Rosemarie Valente
Second Grade Teacher
Newark, New Jersey

Laura A. Holzheimer
Title 1 Reading Teacher
Grades 1–3
Cleveland, Ohio

Sophia Finger, Ed.D.
Assistant Principal
New York, New York

Kelly Johnston Hackett
Instructional Technology
Consultant
Orlando, Florida

Karen Jalowiec Losh
Fort Wayne, Indiana

Acknowledgements

Every good faith effort has been made to locate the owners of copyrighted material to arrange permissions to reprint selections. In several cases this has proved impossible. The publisher will be pleased to consider necessary adjustments for future printings for any owner whose rights may have been unintentionally infringed.

Thanks to the following for permission to reprint the copyrighted materials reprinted below:

"A Friend" (text only) by Betsy Jones Michael, reprinted with permission of the author.

"Trees" A Poem (text only) by Harry Behn. A Bill Martin Book published by Henry Holt and Company. Copyright 1949 Harry Behn. © Renewed 1977 Alice L. Behn. Used by permission of Marian Reiner.

Product Development and Management: Leslie A. Baranowski

"City Street" (text only) by Lois Lenski © 1954 from WE LIVE IN THE CITY. Reprinted with permission of The Lois Lenski Covey Foundation.

"The Museum Door" (text only) by Lee Bennett Hopkins, reprinted by permission of Curtis Brown, Ltd. Copyright © 1987 by Lee Bennett Hopkins.

"What Is Brown?" (text only), from HAILSTONES AND HALIBUT BONES by Mary O'Neill and Leonard Weisgard, Ill. Copyright © 1961 by Mary LeDuc O'Neill. Used by permission of Doubleday, a division of Bantam Doubleday Dell Publishing Group, Inc.

Letter models in this program were used with permission of the publisher, Zaner-Bloser, Inc., Columbus, OH. From HANDWRITING: A WAY TO SELF EXPRESSION, copyright, 1993.

Photo Credits

Neal Farris: Cover

Diane J. Ali: 177 *center.*
Animals Animals/ Earth Scenes—
Richard Shiell: 147 *top;*
E. R. Degginger: 147 *bottom center & top left;*
Robert Maier: 147 *left.*
The Art Institute of Chicago/ photograph ©1995, All rights reserved: 89 *left.*
Cate Photography: 24, 104, 127, 209, 210.
Valerie Henschel: 212 *bottom right.*
Ken Karp: 15 *bottom,* 177 *left.*

Kohout Productions/ Root Resources: 147 *top right.*
Richard Nowitz: 89 *right.*
R. Pasley/ Viesti Associates: 87 *right.*
The Picture Cube/ D. & I. MacDonald: 211 *bottom left;* John Coletti: 219 *top right;* Emily Stone: 223 *top right;* Stanley Rown: 224 *left.*
H. Armstrong Roberts: 34, 65 *right,* 117, 118 *top,* 147 *bottom right,* 147 *bottom left,* 177 *bottom right,* 220 *bottom left.*
Kevin Schafer: 211 *bottom right,* 212 *bottom left,* 220 *top left.*

Jeremy Stafford-Deitsch/ Ellis Nature Photo: 219 *bottom left.*
The Stock Market/ Lew Long: 15 *top right;* Roy Morsch: 15 *center right;* ChromoSohm: 65 *left;* Kunio Owaki: 119 *right;* R. Berenholtz: 119 *left;* Peter Vadnai: 118 *background;* Thomas Braise: 223 *top left.*
SUPERSTOCK: 220 *bottom right.*
Thayer Syme/ FPG International: 219 *top left.*
Tony Stone Images/ Ian Murphy: 15 *top left;* David Hiser: 15 *center left;* Don Spiro: 35; Doug Armand: 45

background, 223 *background;* Suzanne & Nick Geary: 45 *right;* Joe Ortner: 87 *center right;* Doris DeWitt: 87 *center left;* Hugh Sitton: 87 *left;* Mark Burnside: 177 *top right;* Hideo Kurihara: 205 *top left;* Bert Sagara: 205 *top right;* Rainer Grosskopf: 205 *bottom;* Terry Vine: 211 *top left;* Peter Timmermans: 212 *top left;* Jeanne Drake: 219 *bottom right;* Chip Henderson: 224 *right.*
Mark Turner: 220 *top right.*
Larry Ulrich Photography: 211 *top right,* 212 *top right.*

Illustrators

Bart Goldman: Cover, Digital Imaging
Dirk Wunderlich: Cover, Illustration

JoLynn Alcorn: 138
Shirley Beckes: 19
Ken Bowser: 149
Jenny Campbell: 40, 52, 67
Nancy Carpenter: 5
Chi Chung: 17
Peter Church: 121
Karen Dugan: 179
Arthur Friedman: 33, 43, 44, 94, 105, 106, 134, 217, 218

Tom Graham: 20, 37
Adam Gordon: 65, 223, 224
Myron Grossman: 77, 117, 118, 144
Laurie Hamilton : 72, 115, 124
Steve Henry: 75
Joan Holub: 23
Megan Jeffery: 82
Andy Levine: 59, 102, 109, 159, 166, 170, 183
Jason Levinson: 28, 50, 55, 60
Patrick Merrill: 89
John Nez: 61, 63, 64

Iva O'Conner: 110
Olivia: 129, 145, 146, 155, 156
Chris Reed: 36
Cindy Rosenheim: 27
Roz Schanzer: 10, 22, 26, 73, 85, 86, 187, 198
Theresa Smith: 47
Sally Springer: 13, 30, 58, 70
Daryl Stevens: 101, 112, 116, 128, 154, 167, 175, 176, 185
Matt Straub: 215, 216
Steve Sullivan: 6, 18, 48, 68, 90,

122, 150, 180
Don Tate: 96, 100, 131, 136, 163, 172, 181, 193, 199
Vicki Wehrman: 213, 214
Jenny Williams: 11, 54
Susan Williams: 114, 203, 204
Toby Williams: 221, 222

Functional art:
Diane Ali, Bateman Illustration, Moffit Cecil, Adam Gordon, Larry Lee, John Quinn, Sintora Regina Vanderhorst

CONTENTS

A Friend

It's fun to have a friend!
Someone to see and stay with
To walk and talk and play with
To laugh and shout HURRAY with
It's fun to have a friend!

We might not even talk!
We might just sit and giggle
Until we wiggle-wiggle
Or leap and jump and jiggle
We might not even talk!

It's fun to have a friend!
To hold a hand and go with
To ask and learn and know with
To sing and dance and grow with
It's fun to have a friend!

Betsy Jones Michael

Critical Thinking

Why is it fun to have a friend?
How can you make new friends?

LESSON 1: Introduction to Initial, Medial, and Final Consonants

Dear Family,

As your child progresses through this unit about friendship, he or she will review the sounds of the consonants. The 21 letters of the alphabet that are consonants are shown below.

● Say the name of each consonant.

Apreciada Familia:

En esta unidad, acerca de la amistad, su niño repasará los sonidos de las consonantes. Las siguientes letras son las 21 consonantes del idioma inglés.

● Pronuncien cada consonante.

● Read the poem "A Friend" on the reverse side.

● Talk about things friends do together. Tell each other what you like most about a good friend.

● Help your child identify some of the consonants in the poem. Ask what sounds they make.

● Lea al niño la poesía, "A Friend" en la página 5.

● Converse con su niño acerca de lo que hacen los amigos cuando están juntos. Cada uno explique lo que le gusta de un buen amigo.

● Repasen las consonantes que aparecen en la poesía. ¿Cómo suenan?

PROJECT

Ask your child to name some of his or her friends. Together make a list of the names. Underline single consonants in each name. Then choose one friend and write, call, or draw him or her.

Carmela
Omar
Lisa
Jason
Karen

PROYECTO

Pida a su niño nombrar a algunos de sus amigos. Después escriban los nombres. Subrayen las consonantes en cada nombre. Luego, escriban una carta, llamen, o dibujen a uno de los amigos.

Say the name of each picture. Write the letter or letters that stand for the beginning consonant sound.

(j) (m) (k) (f) (z) (s)   (r) (b) (qu) (h) (w) (p)

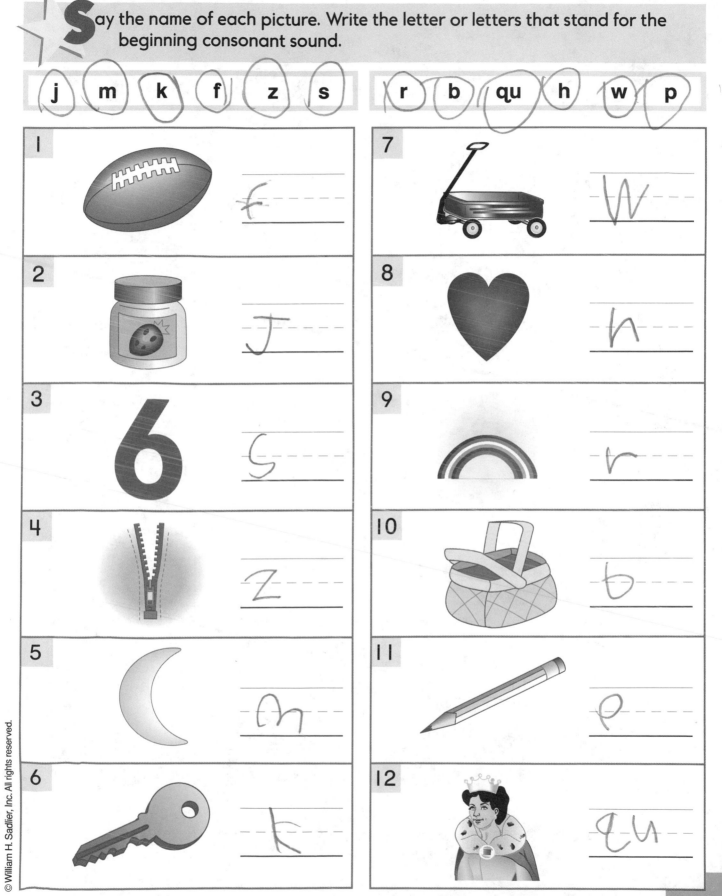

1	f	7	W
2	j	8	h
3	s	9	r
4	z	10	b
5	m	11	p
6	k	12	qu

LESSON 2: Recognizing and Writing Initial Consonants

7

ay the name of each picture. Write the letter that stands for the beginning consonant sound.

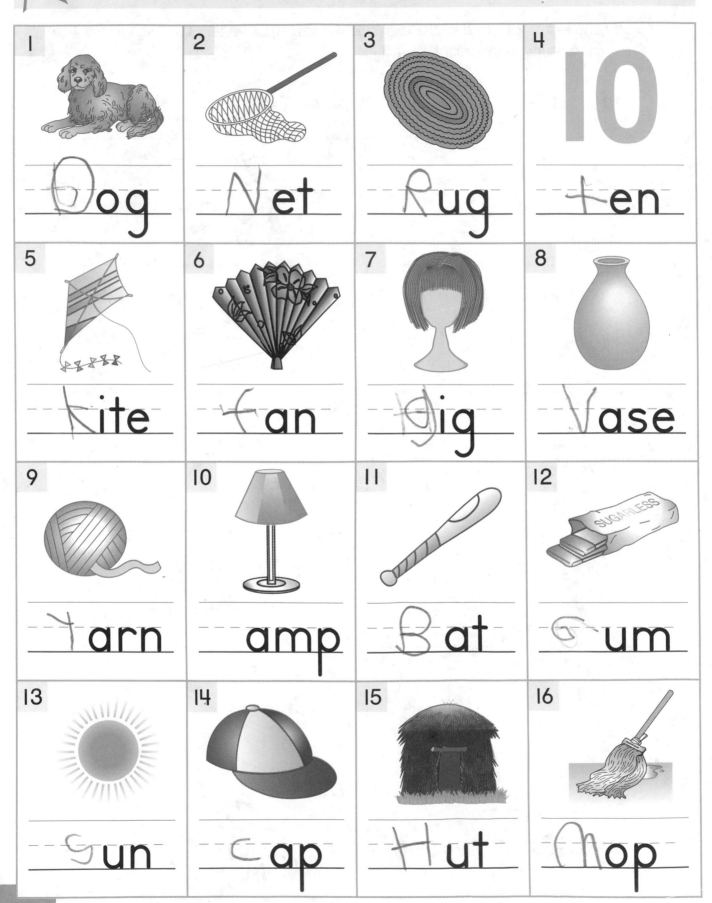

1. Dog
2. Net
3. Rug
4. ten
5. Kite
6. Fan
7. Wig
8. Vase
9. Yarn
10. Lamp
11. Bat
12. Gum
13. Sun
14. Cap
15. Hut
16. Mop

JULIANA RIVELLI

Say the name of each picture. Circle the letter that stands for the ending consonant sound.

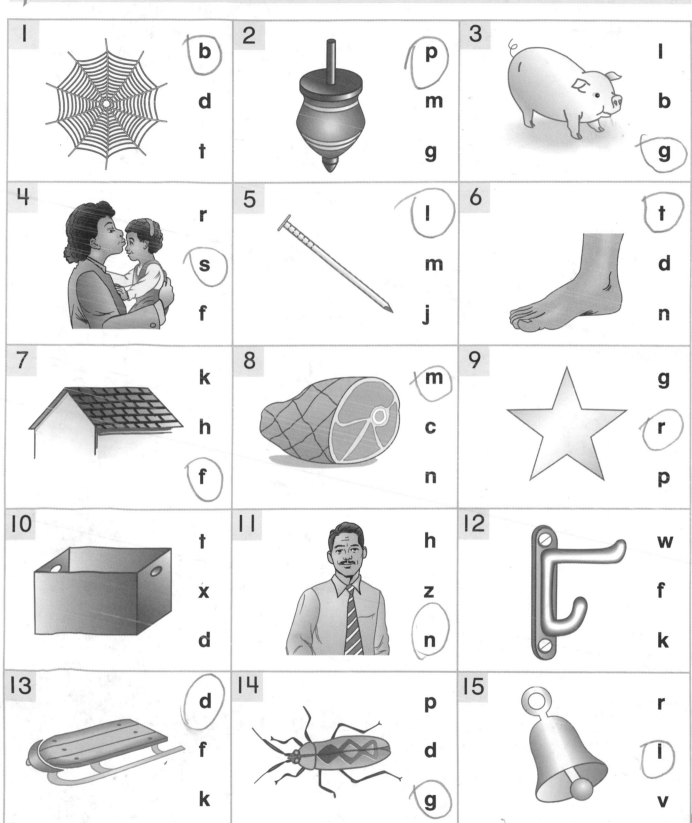

1 (web) — (b) d t	**2** (top) — (p) m g	**3** (pig) — l b (g)
4 (mother) — r (s) f	**5** (nail) — (l) m j	**6** (foot) — (t) d n
7 (roof) — k h (f)	**8** (ham) — (m) c n	**9** (star) — g (r) p
10 (box) — t x d	**11** (man) — h z (n)	**12** (hook) — w f k
13 (sled) — (d) f k	**14** (bug) — p d (g)	**15** (bell) — r (l) v

LESSON 3: Recognizing the Sounds of Final Consonants

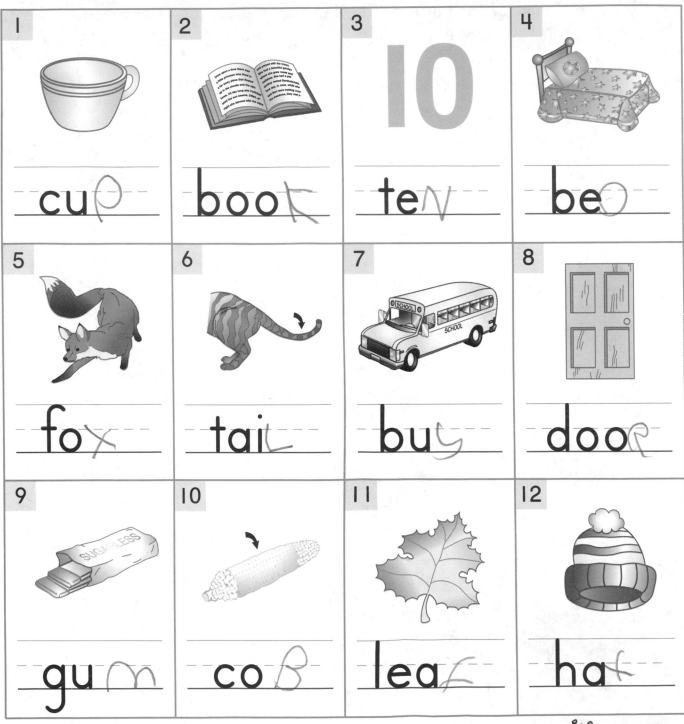

1 cu**p**	2 boo**k**
3 te**n**	4 be**d**
5 fo**x**	6 tai**l**
7 bu**s**	8 doo**r**
9 gu**m**	10 co**b**
11 lea**f**	12 ha**t**

Draw two pictures whose names end like **hat**.
Share your pictures with a partner.

JULIANA RIVELLI

Say the name of each picture. Draw a line from the picture to the letter that stands for the middle consonant sound.

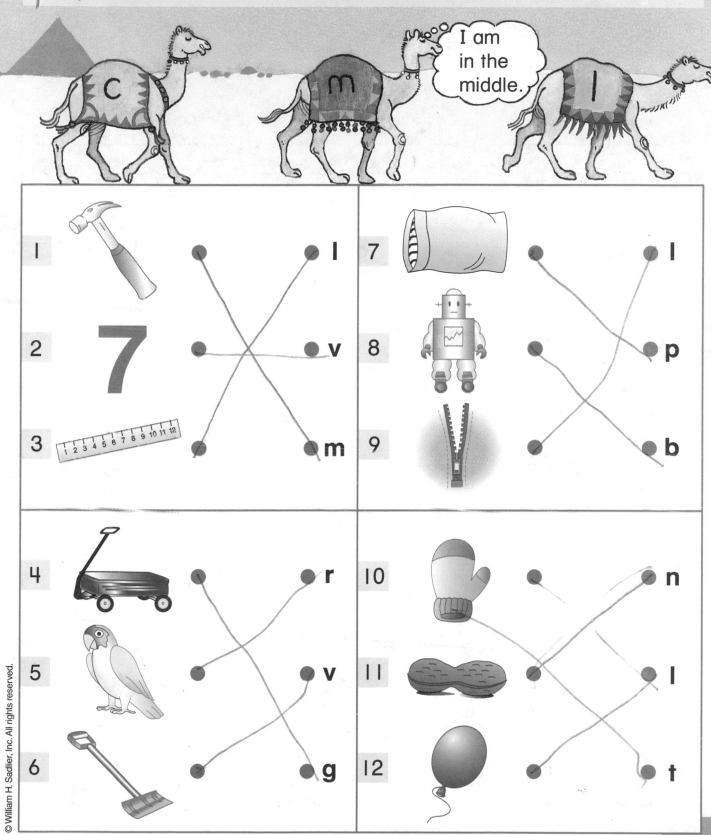

1   •   • l

2   7   •   • v

3   •   • m

7   •   • l

8   •   • p

9   •   • b

4   •   • r

5   •   • v

6   •   • g

10   •   • n

11   •   • l

12   •   • t

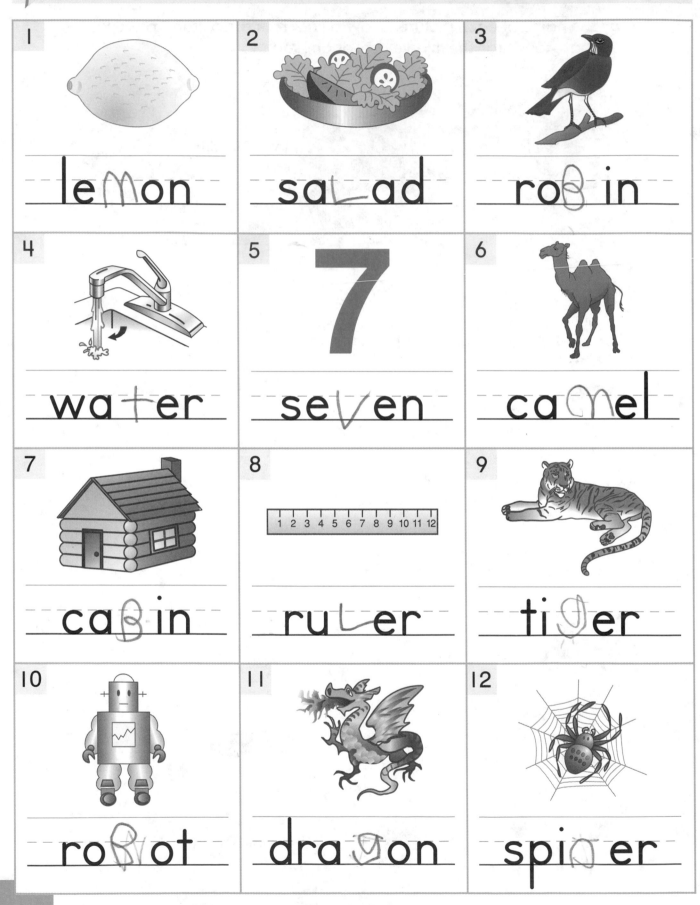

1. le**m**on

2. sa**l**ad

3. ro**b**in

4. wa**t**er

5. se**v**en

6. ca**m**el

7. ca**b**in

8. ru**l**er

9. ti**g**er

10. ro**b**ot

11. dra**g**on

12. spi**d**er

JULI ANA RIVOLLI

Look at the picture clues. Fill in the missing letters in the puzzles.

ACROSS ➡
1
3

DOWN ⬇
1
2

¹C	u	²B		
a		e		
P		³O	o	L L

ACROSS ➡
4 **7**
5
6

DOWN ⬇
4

⁴G	e	v	e	N
a				
⁵L	e	E	o	m
a				
⁶D	o	o	R	

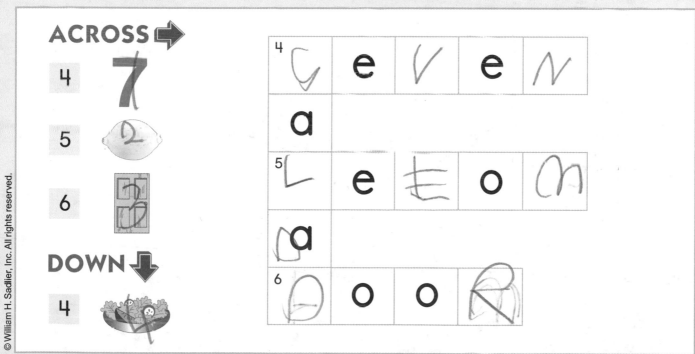

What seven things would you and your friend put in a backpack? Name each thing, and write the letters that stand for the beginning and ending consonant sounds.

LESSON 5: Reviewing Initial, Medial, and Final Consonants

13

Write the missing letter in each picture name. Then find a rhyming word in the box and write it on the line below.

mug · pedal · pig · foxes · pen · hop · van · hat

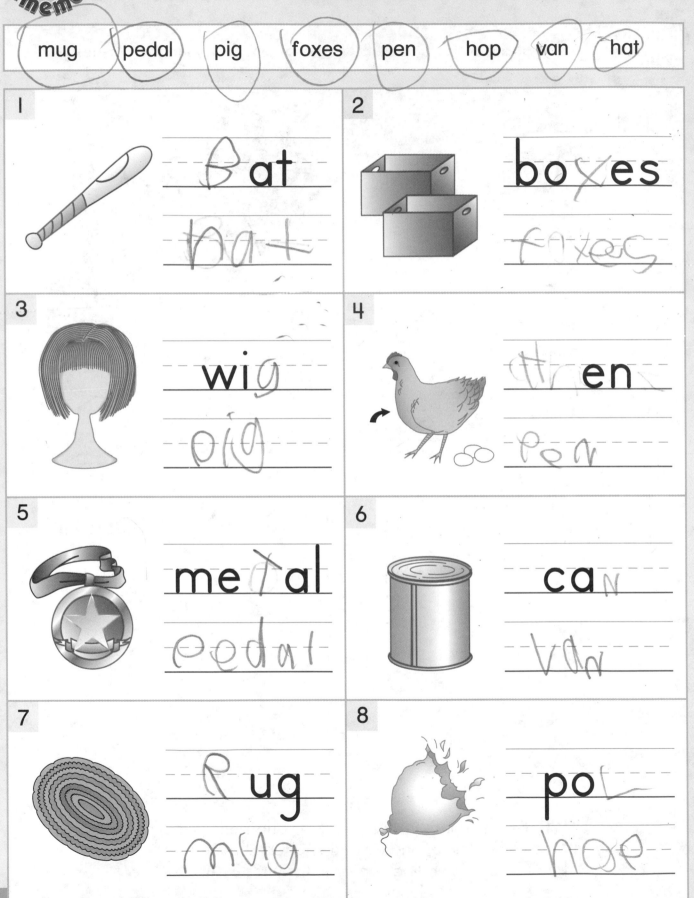

1 Bat
hat

2 boxes
foxes

3 wig
pig

4 hen
pen

5 metal
pedal

6 can
van

7 Rug
mug

8 pot
hop

Look and Learn

Let's read and talk about friendship.

We're best **buddies** in English.
In Spanish we're **amigos**.
Speak French and call us **amis**.
I'll speak Swahili and call you **rafiki**.
You speak Japanese and call
me **tomodachi**.
In any language, we're friends.

How are friends the same all
over the world?

Say the name of each picture. Write the letter that stands for the missing sound.

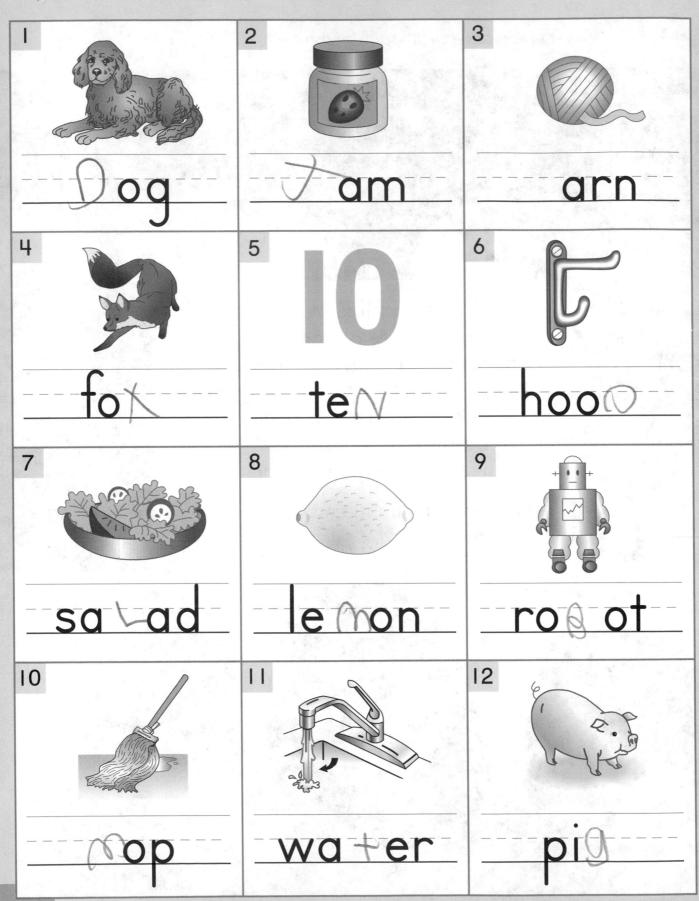

1. _D_og

2. _J_am

3. ___arn

4. fo_x_

5. te_n_

6. hoo_p_

7. sa_l_ad

8. le_m_on

9. ro_b_ot

10. _M_op

11. wa_t_er

12. pi_g_

SAMPAN

Waves lap lap
Fish fins clap clap
Brown sails flap flap
Chop-sticks tap tap
Up and down the long green river
Ohe Ohe lanterns quiver
Willow branches brush the river
Ohe Ohe lanterns quiver
Waves lap lap
Fish fins clap clap
Brown sails flap flap
Chop-sticks tap tap

Tao Lang Pee

Critical Thinking
What sights might you see along a river?
What sounds might you hear?

LESSON 7: Introduction to Short Vowels

JULI ANA RIVOLLT

Dear Family,

As your child progresses through this unit about water and rivers, she or he will review the short vowel sounds of **a, i, o, u,** and **e**.

● Say the picture names and listen to the short vowel sound in the middle of each word.

Apreciada Familia:

En esta unidad, acerca del agua y los ríos, su niño repasará el sonido corto de las vocales **a, i, o, u, e**.

● Pronuncie el nombre de las cosas en los cuadros y escuche el sonido corto de las vocales en cada palabra.

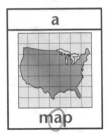
a
map

i
fin

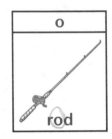
o
rod

u
tug

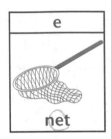
e
net

● Read the poem "Sampan" on the reverse side.

● Talk about what it might be like to live on a boat.

● Point out some of the short vowel words in the poem. (l**a**p, f**i**sh, f**i**ns, cl**a**p, fl**a**p, ch**o**p, st**i**cks, **a**nd, t**a**p, **u**p, br**u**sh)

● Lea a su niño, "Sampan" en la página 17.

● Hablen sobre como sería vivir en un barco.

● Señalen algunas palabras en la poesía donde el sonido de la vocal es corto como: (l**a**p, f**i**sh, f**i**ns, cl**a**p, fl**a**p, ch**o**p, st**i**cks, **a**nd, t**a**p, **u**p, br**u**sh).

PROJECT

On a large sheet of paper, draw a picture of a river. Cut out small pieces of paper in the shape of logs. When your child learns a new short vowel word, have him or her write the word on a log and tape it on the river.

sun
log
fin
bag
pen

PROYECTO

Dibuje un río en un papel grande. Corte pedacitos de papel en forma de tronco. Cuando el niño reconozca una palabra con vocales de sonido corto puede escribirla en un papelito y pegarla en el río.

Read the story. Underline the short **a** words.

What's in the Sand?

There's lots to see and do in the sand.
Pam watches a crab in the sand.
Jan sees an old map in the sand.
Nat prints his hand in the sand.
Dad finds his cap in the sand.
What can you find in the sand?

Look at and say the phonogram at the top of each box. Then circle the two pictures whose names have that phonogram. Write the words.

1   **_b**ag

2   **H**am

3   **_**an

4   **h_a**t

Taking Off

Write a silly sentence with two rhyming words.
Tell what you can take on a raft. For example,
"On my raft I can take a **ram** and a **ham**."

Helpful Hint

If a syllable or word has only one vowel and it comes at the beginning or between two consonants, the vowel usually has the **short** sound.

Map has the short **a** sound. Circle and write the short **a** word that names each picture. In the last box, draw a picture of a short **a** word. Write the word.

1		2		3	
	mat		bad		(fan)
	(map)		tag		tan
	cat		(bag)		fat

4		5		6	
	fad		(gas)		yam
	cap		sag		(jam)
	(cab)		gap		ram

7		8		9	
	(hand)		tax		
	land		(tag)		
	sand		(wax)		

Look at the picture. Circle and write the word that completes the sentence.

1

Dad and Sam __pack__ lunch.

tack
(pack)
tap

2

They load the __van__.

(van)
yam
man

3

Dad stops for a __map__.

pan
nap
(map)

4

The map leads to the __cap__.

lamp
(camp)
cap

5

Sam sees a __fat__ beaver.

fad
pal
(fat)

6

It __Has__ a flat tail.

pass
hat
(has)

7

It swims very __fast__!

(fast)
sat
cast

LESSON 9: Short Vowel **a** in Sentences

Read the poem. Underline the short **i** words. Then use short **i** words to complete the sentences.

Swish, Swish, Swish

Bill and Jill will never miss
A chance to see the giant fish.
Up and down the big fish swim.
Watch their fins go swish, swish, swish.

What a thrill for Jill and Bill
To see the colorful fish!
In and out the big fish swim.
Watch their fins go swish, swish, swish.

1. Bill and Jill see giant _____fish_____.

2. The big fish _____swim_____ up and down.

3. The fish swim _____swish_____ and out.

4. The fins of the fish go swish, swish, _____swish_____.

1

pig
big

pig

2

kit
hit

kit

3

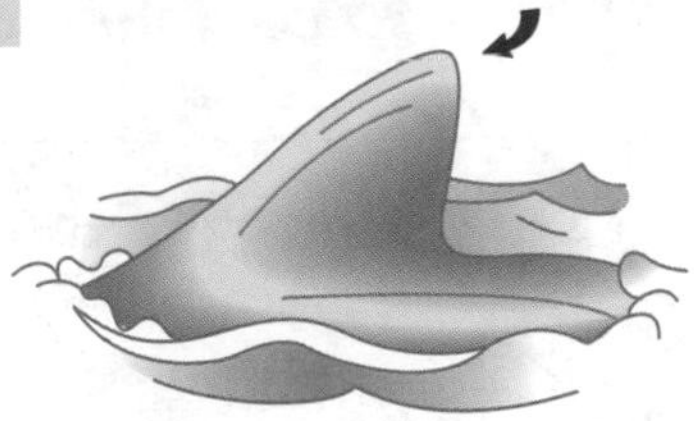

fin
bin

fih

4

lid
bid

lid

5

hill
fill

Hill

6

kick
lick

kick

Talking Off

Work with a partner. Write a list of words that rhyme with **k**ing.

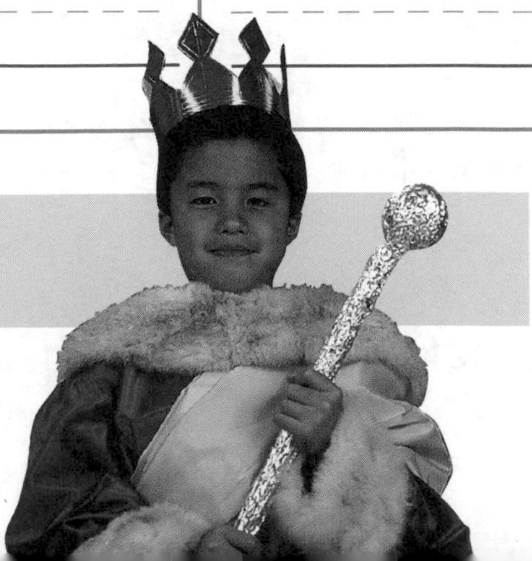

Fin has the short **i** sound. Find the name of each picture. Write the word.

hill	ring	fin	list	bib	six
pink	kiss	milk	rip	lid	mitt

1

fin

2

lid

3

milk

4

bib

5

Hill

6

kiss

7

rip

8

pink

9

mitt

10

six

11

ring

12

list

LESSON 11: Recognizing and Writing Short Vowel **i**

25

Fill in the circle before the sentence that tells about the picture.

1. ● Kit will learn to swim.
    ○ Kit will learn to wink.

2. ○ She sips her milk fast.
    ● She kicks her feet fast.

3. ○ Will Kit sit well?
    ● Will Kit swim well?

4. ● Ms. Hill gives Kit a tip.
    ○ Ms. Hill gives Kit a wig.

5. ○ Now Kit can sniff like a fish.
    ● Now Kit can swish like a fish.

6. ● Kit sits down to rest.
    ○ Kit rests on a hill.

7. ○ Ms. Hill has a list for Kit.
    ● Ms. Hill has a gift for Kit.

Taking Off

Draw a picture about swimming. Write one sentence that goes with the picture and one that does not. Ask someone to choose the correct sentence.

Read the poem. Underline the short **o** words. Then use short **o** words to complete the sentences.

At the Pond

Tom went to the pond,
And he sat on some rocks.
He put bait on his rod.
Then he took off his socks.

Tom saw a frog on a log.
He said, "Please don't hop.
You'll scare the fish
If you don't stop."

1. Tom went to the _____ .

2. He took off his _____ .

3. There was a _____ on a log.

4. Tom asked the frog not to _____ .

Look at and say the phonogram at the top of each box. Then circle the two pictures whose names have that phonogram. Write the words.

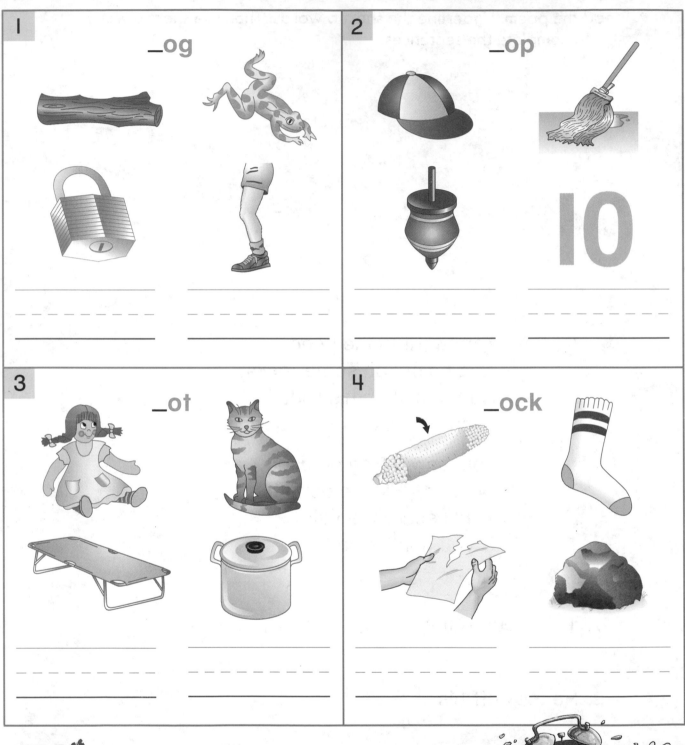

1. _og

2. _op

3. _ot

4. _ock

Write a silly sentence with two rhyming words. Tell what you saw at the pond. For example, "At the pond I saw a wet **clock** on a **rock**."

Rod has the short **o** sound. Circle and write the short **o** word that names each picture. In the last box, draw a picture of a short **o** word. Write the word.

1 rob / cod / rod	**2** tot / mop / top	**3** nod / cob / job
4 box / fox / frog	**5** tock / rot / rock	**6** doll / dot / dock
7 pod / pop / pot	**8** cop / cot / not	**9** log / fog / lot
10 plot / fond / pond	**11** lot / lock / clock	**12**

Write complete sentences. Put the last three words in order.

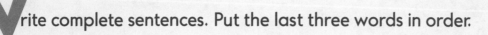

1

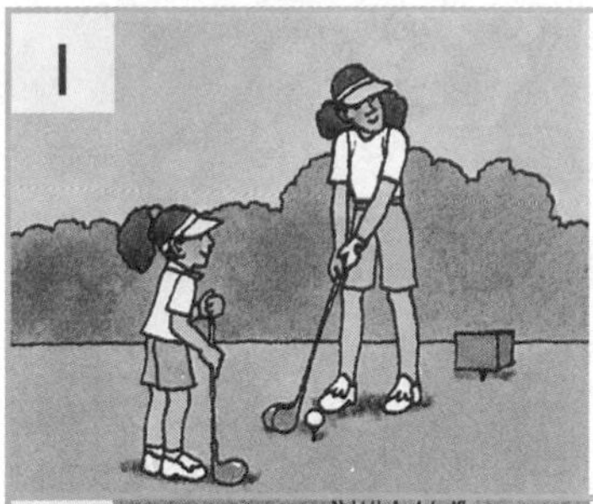

to like golf

Mom and Anita ______________________.

2

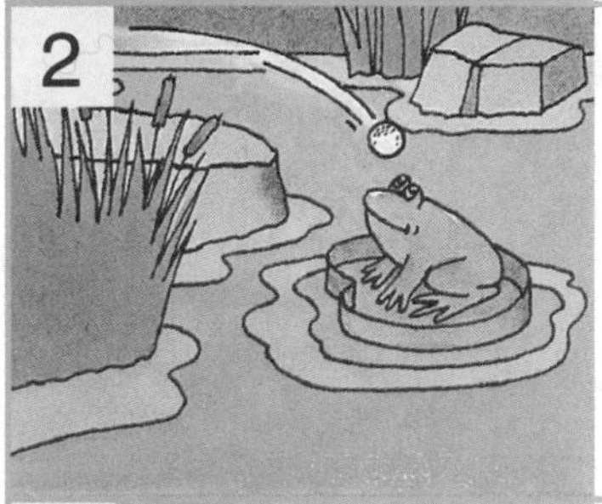

a pond into

Mom hit the ball ______________________.

3

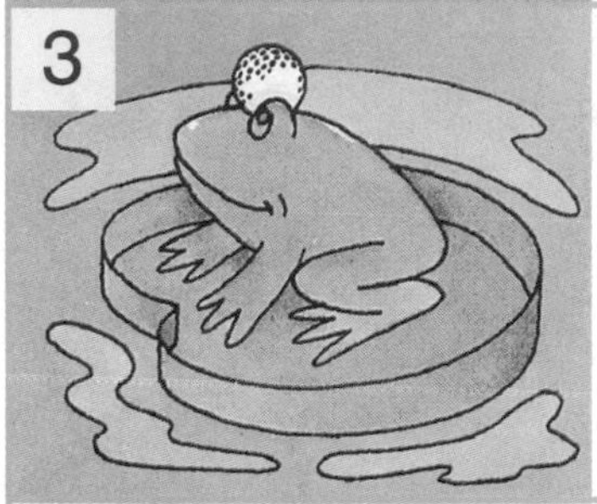

frog on a

They saw it land ______________________.

4

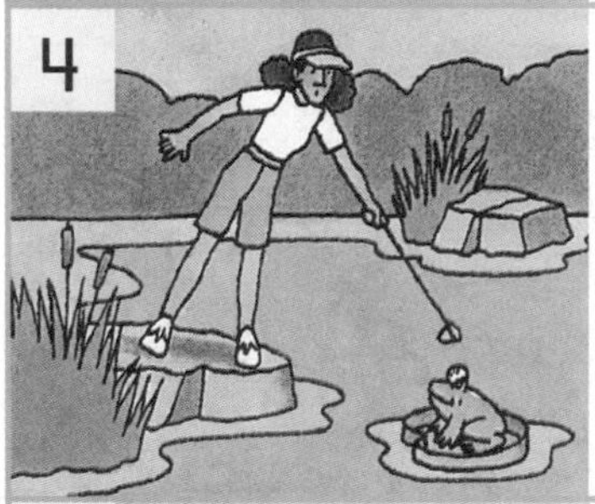

off rock the

"Mom, don't slip ______________________."

5

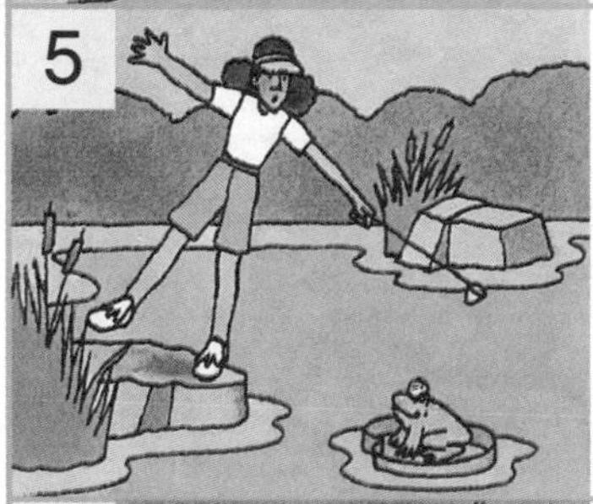

stop not did

But Mom ______________________.

6

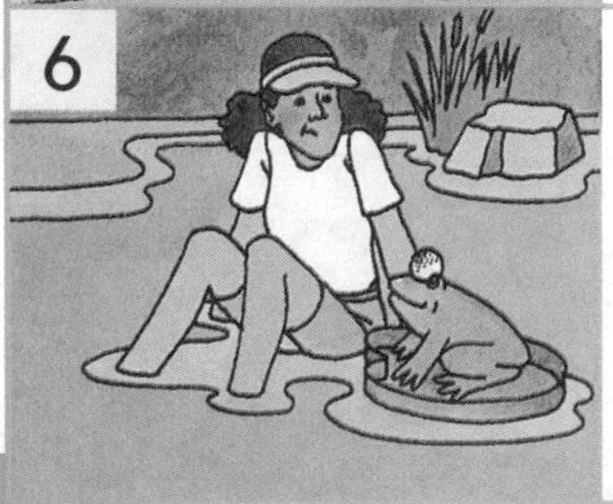

a with plop

She fell in ______________________!

Draw a line through three boxes in a row with words or pictures that have the same vowel sound. You can go across, down, or corner-to-corner.

1

map		
	job	pop
ham	lip	zip

2

trip		win
log		sag
	pot	hit

3

	log	band
	hot	
bit	sing	sag

4

	bill	
mitt	back	fad
mop	rob	

Write a short story. Pretend you're at a fishing pond with a friend. What happens there? Use some of these words in your story: **pal, sand, map, swim, wind, fish, rock, fog, dock**.

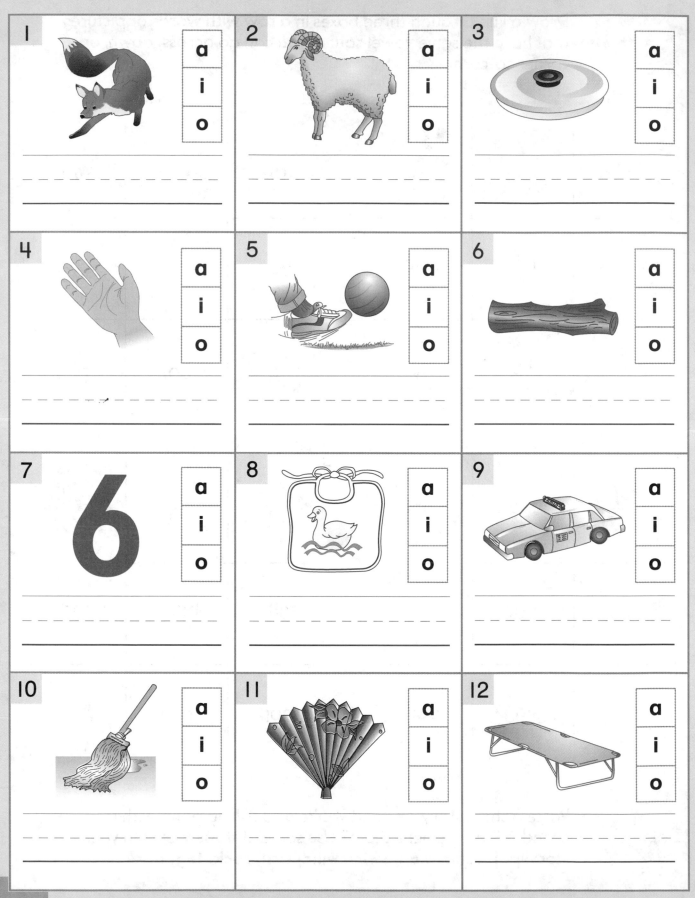

Read the poem. Underline the short **u** words. Then use short **u** words to complete the sentences.

Here Comes the Tug!

I have a friend named Rusty.
He has a boat named Dusty.
Up and down the river she runs,
Giving free rides, just for fun.

Oh no, Rusty. What's that thud?
It's poor Dusty, stuck in mud.
Rusty, get the boat to run,
Or we'll sit here in the sun.

Don't fuss, Rusty. We're in luck.
Dusty soon will be unstuck.
Listen and you'll hear a chug.
Aren't you glad to see the tug?

1. Rusty's boat is named _____.

2. Dusty went _____ and down the river.

3. The boat got _____ in the mud.

4. The _____ came to help.

Say the name of each picture. Then read the words. Look at the phonogram in the words and write two more words with that phonogram.

1

bug
mug

_____
_____
_____

2

cut
hut

_____
_____
_____

3

sun
fun

_____
_____
_____

4

cub
tub

_____
_____
_____

5

drum
sum

_____
_____
_____

6

trunk
bunk

_____
_____
_____

Talking Off

Work with a partner. Write a list of words that rhyme with **st**ump.

Tug has the short **u** sound. Write the name of each short **u** picture.

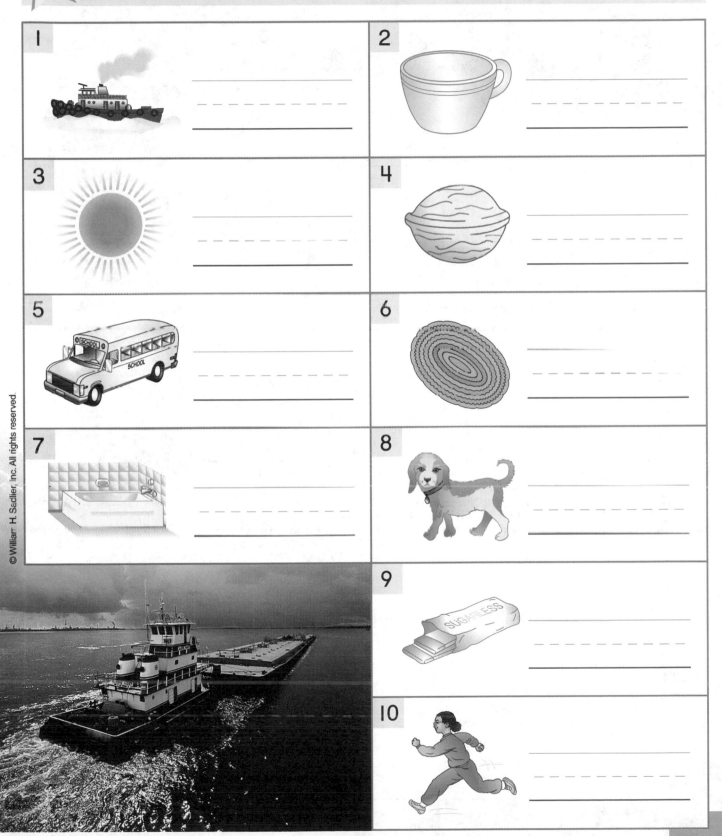

1

2

3

4

5

6

7

8

9

10

Use a word from the box to complete each sentence.
Then read the story.

| bumps | gulls | hums | run | stuff |

Lucky Gus

Gus likes to _____ on the

beach. He _____ a song

as he jogs. He waves at the _____

in the sky. He looks for _____

in the sand.

One day Gus _____ into

a trunk. Lucky Gus!

What do you think Gus finds in the trunk?
Write about it.

_____

_____

Read the poem. Underline the short **e** words. Then look at the pictures to answer the question.

At the Shore

Kara sells shells.
Sam mends nets.
Tess draws pictures.
Jen walks pets.

Ed sells fresh fish.
Jet takes a nap.
Ben rents rowboats.
Ken gets a snack.

Who gets wet?

_____

_____

LESSON 17: Introduction to Short Vowel **e**   **37**

Say the name of each picture. Look at the phonogram in the picture name and write another word with that phonogram.

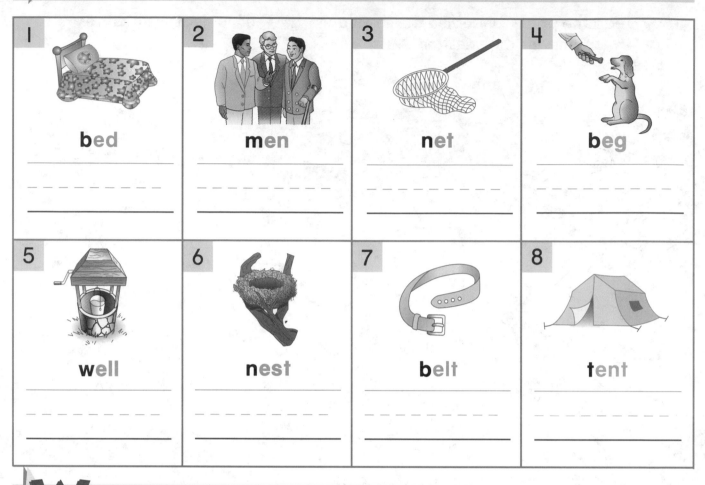

1	2	3	4
bed	**men**	**net**	**beg**

5	6	7	8
well	**nest**	**belt**	**tent**

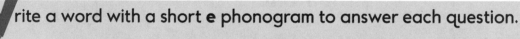 **W**rite a word with a short **e** phonogram to answer each question.

9. What names a color and rhymes with **bed**?

10. What names a number and rhymes with **men**?

11. What gives you water and rhymes with **bell**?

12. What holds your pants up and rhymes with **melt**?

Wet has the short **e** sound. Find the name of each picture.
Write the word.

well	vest	web	wet	desk	leg
jet	ten	hen	belt	sled	egg

1.

2.

3.

4.

5.

6.

7.

8.

9.

10.

11.

12.

Fill in the circle before the sentence that tells about the picture.

1. ○ Ming wears a dress.
   ○ Ming wears a vest.

2. ○ She goes on deck.
   ○ She goes to bed.

3. ○ Chen helps fix the desk.
   ○ Chen helps mend the net.

4. ○ Ming gets ten fish.
   ○ Ming gets six eggs.

5. ○ They sell the last nest to Jen.
   ○ They sell the best fish to Jen.

6. ○ The rest are fed to the gulls.
   ○ The rest are led to the tent.

7. ○ Ming and Chen get wet.
   ○ Ming and Chen go to the vet.

Draw a picture of Ming and Chen. Write one sentence that goes with the picture and one that does not. Ask someone to choose the correct sentence.

Unscramble the words to make sentences. Write each sentence.

1 into a puddle. Nell fell

_____

2 very Nell wet. got

_____

3 in water. Ducks day spend all

_____

4 They ponds. jump into and puddles

_____

5 bugs hunt for They under water.

_____

6 lucky. are ducks But

_____

7 do not Ducks wet! get

_____

Color the box that contains the short vowel sound in each picture name. Write the word.

1. | u |
| e |

_____

2. | u |
| e |

_____

3. | u |
| e |

_____

4. | u |
| e |

_____

5. | u |
| e |

_____

6. | u |
| e |

_____

7. | u |
| e |

_____

8. | u |
| e |

_____

9. | u |
| e |

_____

10. | u |
| e |

_____

11. | u |
| e |

_____

12. | u |
| e |

_____

42   LESSON 19: Assessing Short Vowels **u** and **e**

Spell and Write Say and spell each word in the box. Then write each word under the short vowel sound in its name.

big	
cut	
ran	
ten	
got	
tug	
let	
did	
fox	
has	

1 Short **a**

2 Short **i**

3 Short **o**

4 Short **u**

5 Short **e**

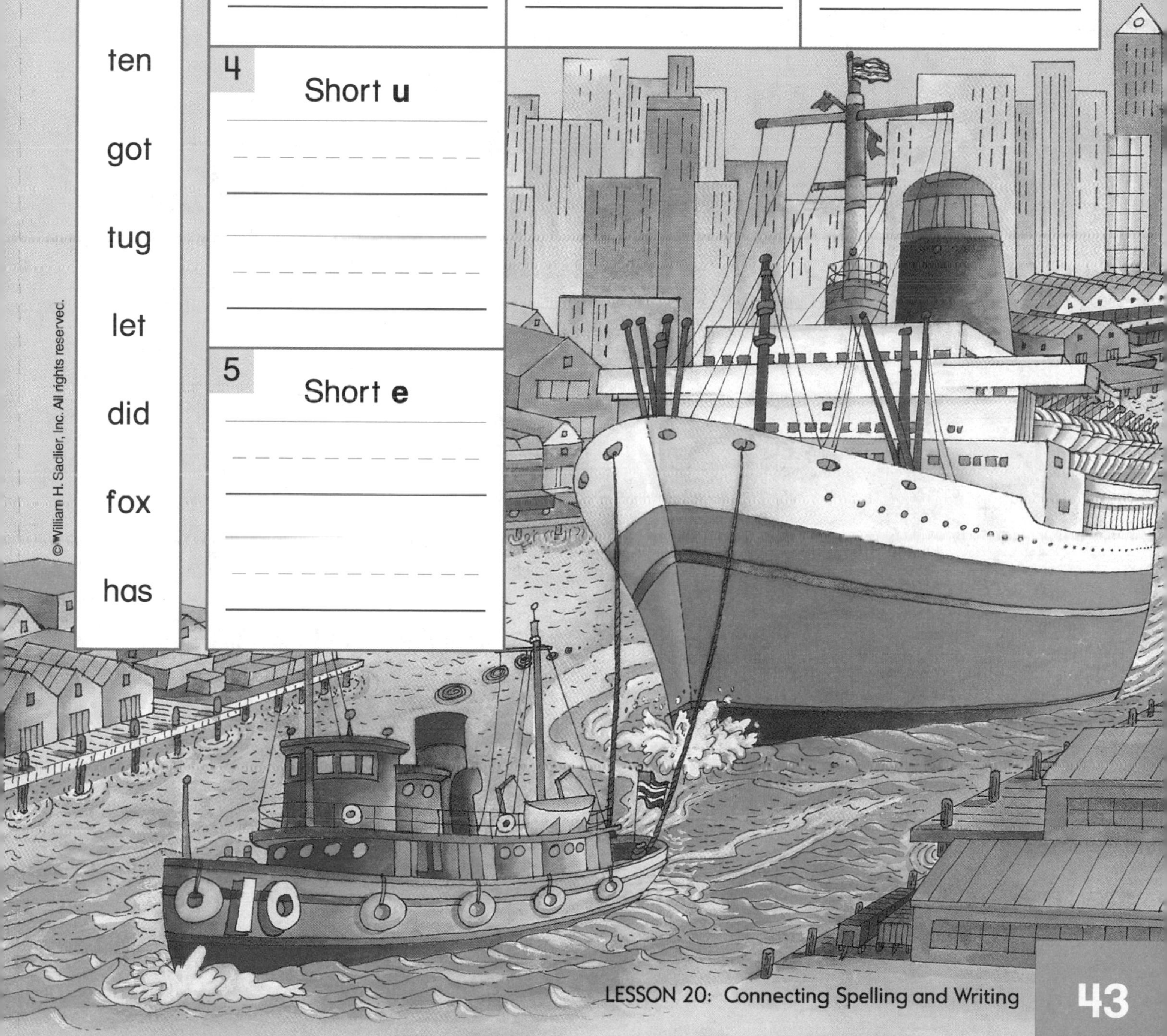

 **Spell and Write**

The pictures tell a story. Draw a picture to show what happens next. Then write a sentence to go with each picture. Use one or more of your spelling words.

big	cut	ran	ten	got	tug	let	did	fox	has

1

_____

_____

_____

_____

_____

2

_____

_____

_____

_____

3

_____

_____

_____

_____

_____

Look and Learn

Let's read and talk about Niagara Falls.

Welcome to Niagara Falls. These falls are in New York and in Canada. Do you want to see the top? Visit the tower on the New York side. Watch the water rush down with a crash.

Would you like a closer look? Put on a raincoat and take a boat ride on the *Maid of the Mist*. But don't get upset if you get wet!

If you visited Niagara Falls, what would you do there?

 **Fill in the circle next to the word that names the picture.**

1
- ○ fun
- ○ fan
- ○ fin

2
- ○ big
- ○ bag
- ○ bug

3
- ○ pig
- ○ pug
- ○ peg

4
- ○ leg
- ○ lag
- ○ log

5
- ○ bud
- ○ bed
- ○ bid

6
- ○ not
- ○ nut
- ○ net

7
- ○ list
- ○ lost
- ○ last

eggs
bread
milk
juice
apples

8
- ○ hum
- ○ him
- ○ ham

9
- ○ wall
- ○ will
- ○ well

10
- ○ cab
- ○ cub
- ○ cob

11
- ○ led
- ○ lad
- ○ lid

12
- ○ sock
- ○ sick
- ○ sack

13
- ○ tan
- ○ tin
- ○ ten

10

14
- ○ tap
- ○ top
- ○ tip

15
- ○ hit
- ○ hut
- ○ hat

3

TREES

Trees are the kindest things I know,
They do no harm, they simply grow

And spread a shade for sleepy cows,
And gather birds among their boughs.

They give us fruit in leaves above,
And wood to make our houses of,

And leaves to burn on Hallowe'en,
And in the Spring new buds of green.

They are the first when day's begun
To touch the beams of morning sun,

They are the last to hold the light
When evening changes into night,

And when a moon floats on the sky
They hum a drowsy lullaby

Of sleepy children long ago . . .
Trees are the kindest things I know.

Harry Behn

Critical Thinking
In what other ways are trees kind?
What can you do to be kind to trees?

Dear Family,

As your child progresses through this unit about trees and nature, he or she will review the long vowel sounds of **a**, **i**, **o**, **u**, and **e**.

● Say the picture names and listen to the long vowel sounds. Long vowels say their own names.

Apreciada Familia:

En esta unidad, acerca de la naturaleza, su niño repasará los sonidos largos de las vocales **a, i, o, u, e**.

● Pronuncie el nombre de las cosas y escuche el sonido largo de las vocales. El sonido largo es como el nombre de la vocal.

a	i	o	u	e

rain	vine	snow	fruit	leaf

● Read the poem "Trees" on the reverse side.

● Talk about different ways that trees help us.

● Point out some of the long vowel words in the poem. (**tre̲e̲s**, **kn̲o̲w**, **gr̲o̲w**, **sh̲a̲de̲**, **sl̲e̲epy**, **fr̲u̲it**, **l̲e̲ave̲s**, **m̲a̲ke̲**, **gr̲e̲en**, **be̲a̲ms**, **fl̲o̲a̲ts**)

● Lea la poesía "Trees" en la página 47.

● Hable con su niño sobre cómo los árboles nos ayudan.

● Señalen algunas palabras donde el sonido de la vocal es largo como: (**tre̲e̲s**, **kn̲o̲w**, **gr̲o̲w**, **sh̲a̲de̲**, **sl̲e̲epy**, **fr̲u̲it**, **l̲e̲ave̲s**, **m̲a̲ke̲**, **gr̲e̲en**, **be̲a̲ms**, **fl̲o̲a̲ts**).

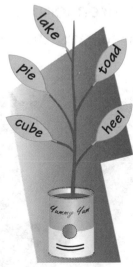

PROJECT

Make a word tree from a small branch that has fallen off a tree. Fill an empty can with dirt or clay, and put the branch in the can so that it stands up. Then have your child draw leaves and cut them out. He or she can write new long vowel words on the leaves and attach them to the tree.

PROYECTO

Haga un árbol de palabras. Consiga una ramita de un árbol. Llene una lata de tierra o barro para sostener la rama. Haga que el niño dibuje hojas y las recorte. A medida que el niño vaya aprendiendo palabras donde el sonido de las vocales es largo, puede escribirlas en las hojas y atarlas al árbol con un cordón.

Circle the long **a** word that names each picture.

1 lake lap	2 ran rain	3 ham hay
4 gate tag	5 pal pail	6 jay jam

Say the phonogram at the beginning of each row. Circle the words with that phonogram. Then write another word with the same phonogram.

7	_ake	rake	ran	lake	_____
8	_ain	pan	pain	rain	_____
9	_ay	hay	way	wag	_____
10	_ate	late	gate	tag	_____
11	_ail	map	mail	pail	_____

If there are two vowels in a one-syllable word, the first vowel is usually **long** and the second vowel is silent. There are different ways to spell long vowels.

Lake, **rain,** and **hay** have the long **a** sound. Color the raindrops that have long **a** words.

came
cab
pave
late
gain
wait
tan
way
sail
may
mat
tap
say
make
lane

Circle and write the word that completes each sentence.

1. Fay likes to _____ on rainy days.   paint   pan

2. She paints a picture of the _____ sky.   grass   gray

3. She also likes to make things with _____ .   clam   clay

4. She makes a horse with a long _____ .   man   mane

5. One day she _____ take art classes.   may   mat

Circle the word that names each picture. Color the pictures whose names have the long **i** sound.

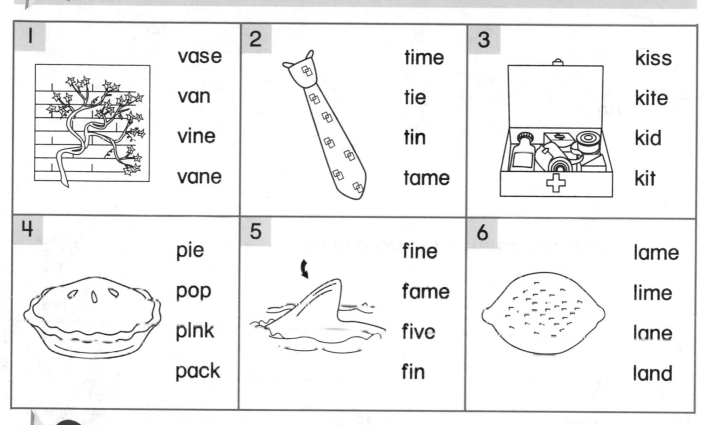

1		2		3	
	vase		time		kiss
	van		tie		kite
	vine		tin		kid
	vane		tame		kit

4		5		6	
	pie		fine		lame
	pop		fame		lime
	plnk		fivc		lane
	pack		fin		land

Say each phonogram. Then read the words. Write another word with the same phonogram.

7	8	9	10
_ine	_ie	_ime	_ide
vine	tie	dime	hide
dine	lie	time	side
_____	_____	_____	_____
_____	_____	_____	_____
_____	_____	_____	_____

Work with a partner. Write a list of words that rhyme with **b**ike.

LESSON 24: Long Vowel **i** Phonograms

Vine and **tie** have the long **i** sound. Change each word to a long **i** word by adding a final **e**.

1 kit	2 rip	3 pin	4 fin
5 rid	6 dim	7 hid	8 bit

Use a word from above to complete each phrase.

9. _____ a bike

10. fly a _____

11. nickel and _____

12. a _____ day

13. a _____ plum

14. a _____ tree

15. _____ and seek

16. a big _____

Circle the long **o** word that names each picture.

1 raise rise rose	**2** bat boat bone	**3** snail snow slow
4 road robe rod	**5** can cane cone	**6** smoke smile snake

Say the phonogram at the beginning of each row. Circle the words with that phonogram. Then write another word with the same phonogram.

7	_ose	pass	hose	nose	_____
8	_oat	boat	cot	coat	_____
9	_ow	row	mow	mop	_____
10	_one	bone	cone	bake	_____
11	_oke	wake	woke	poke	_____

Rose, boat, and snow have the long o sound. Color the stones that have long o words.

home   low   dock   soak   note   sock

roam   block   woke   tone   doll   hose

blow   foam   stop   zone   rode   rock

The underlined word in each sentence does not make sense. Write a long o word from the box that would make sense.

bow	cone	rose	toad	rope	loaf

1. I have ice cream in a <u>cane</u>. _____

2. Joe tied the boat with a <u>rake</u>. _____

3. Ben has a <u>lime</u> of bread in a bag. _____

4. Mike put a <u>bike</u> on the gift. _____

5. A red <u>ride</u> grows in the garden. _____

6. Mom saw a <u>tide</u> jump in the lake. _____

Look at the picture. Then follow the directions below.

Directions

1. Color the lake blue.
2. Draw a road by the lake.
3. Circle the boat.
4. Color the pine tree green.
5. Draw a box around the kite.
6. Color each rose yellow.

7. Color the pail gray.
8. Draw a hole for the mole.
9. Draw a line over the stone.
10. Make an X on the hive.
11. Color the toad brown.
12. Draw a tail on the fox.

Color the box that contains the long vowel sound in each picture name. Write the word.

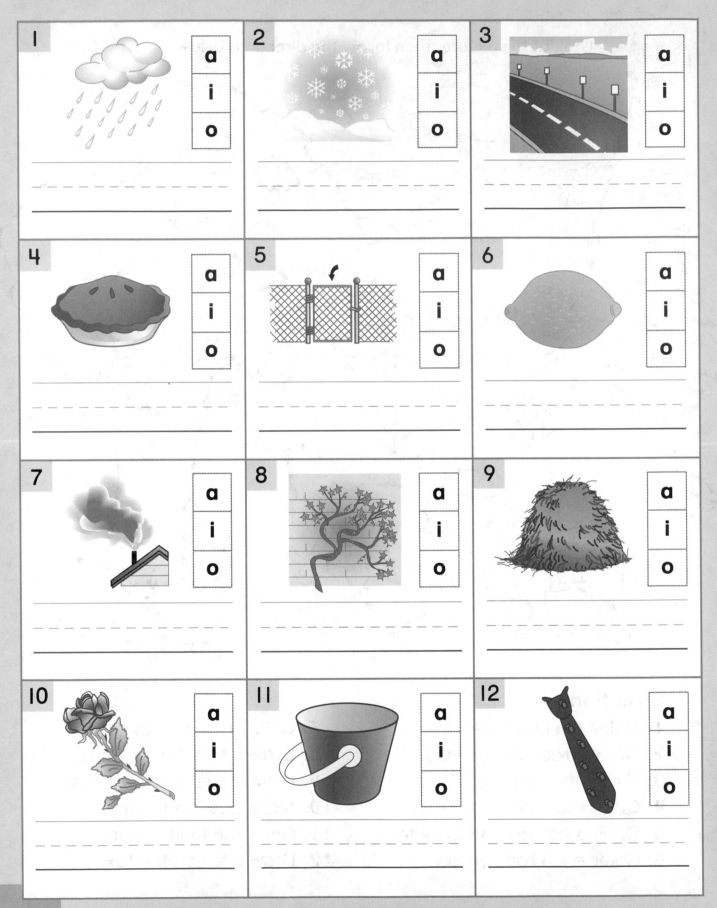

1 a i o	2 a i o	3 a i o
4 a i o	5 a i o	6 a i o
7 a i o	8 a i o	9 a i o
10 a i o	11 a i o	12 a i o

Find the name of each long **u** picture. Write the word.

| mule | tune | tube | glue | suit | blue | fruit | flute |

1		2	
3		4	
5		6	
7		8	

Read each word. Then make a new word with the same phonogram.
Write the phonogram next to the letter or letters on the line.

9 **t**ube	10 **fr**uit	11 **bl**ue	12 **t**une
c	s	cl	d

LESSON 27: Long Vowel **u** Phonograms

57

Tube, fruit, and blue have the long **u** sound. Complete each sentence by choosing two long **u** words that make sense.

1

fruit   cube   juice

_____   _____

- - - - - - - - - -   - - - - - - - - - -

Sue makes _____ _____.

2

mule   dune   cute

_____   _____

- - - - - - - - - -   - - - - - - - - - -

Joe rides a _____ _____.

3

fuse   flute   tune

_____   _____

- - - - - - - - - -   - - - - - - - - - -

June plays a _____ on a _____.

4

huge   tuba   rule

_____   _____

- - - - - - - - - -   - - - - - - - - - -

Duke plays a _____ _____.

5

suit   clue   blue

- - - - - - - - - -   - - - - - - - - - -

_____   _____

Luke gets a new _____ _____.

6

due   use   ruler

_____   _____

- - - - - - - - - -   - - - - - - - - - -

Nina likes to _____ a _____.

Circle the long **e** word that names each picture.

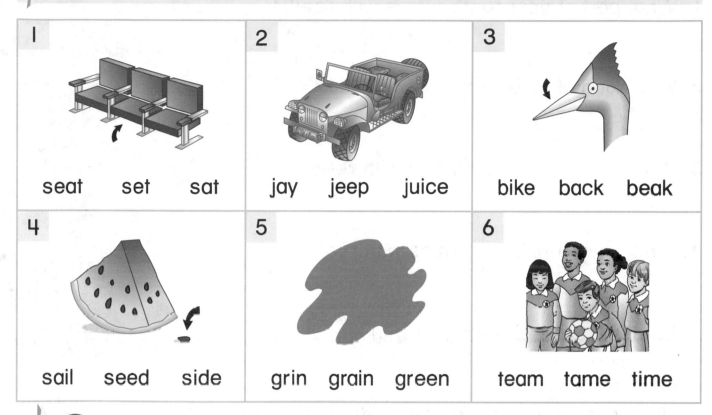

1 seat set sat	**2** jay jeep juice	**3** bike back beak
4 sail seed side	**5** grin grain green	**6** team tame time

Say each phonogram. Then read the words. Write another word with the same phonogram.

7 _eam	8 _eep	9 _eed	10 _eak
beam cream	creep deep	feed need	leak speak
_____	_____	_____	_____
_____	_____	_____	_____

Write a silly question that begins "Have you ever **seen**...?" For example, "Have you ever **seen** a **tree** of **green beans**?"

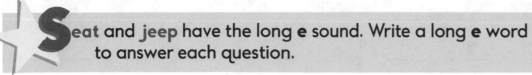

Seat and **jeep** have the long **e** sound. Write a long **e** word to answer each question.

1. What part of your foot rhymes with **feel**? _____

2. What kind of insect rhymes with **see**? _____

3. What part of a plant rhymes with **reed**? _____

4. What kind of animal rhymes with **real**? _____

5. What part of a bird rhymes with **leak**? _____

6. What part of a month rhymes with **peek**? _____

Change the vowel in each word to **ea** to write a new word. Read the new long **e** word.

7 not	8 bat	9 trot
10 mat	11 stem	12 drum

Combine words from boxes 1, 2, and 3 to write sentences. How many different sentences can you write?

1	2	3
Sweet Sue Queen Jean Mr. Green	plays the flute rides a mule plants a tree	on a dune. each June. on the street.

 **Check-Up** Color the box that contains the long vowel sound in each picture name. Write the word.

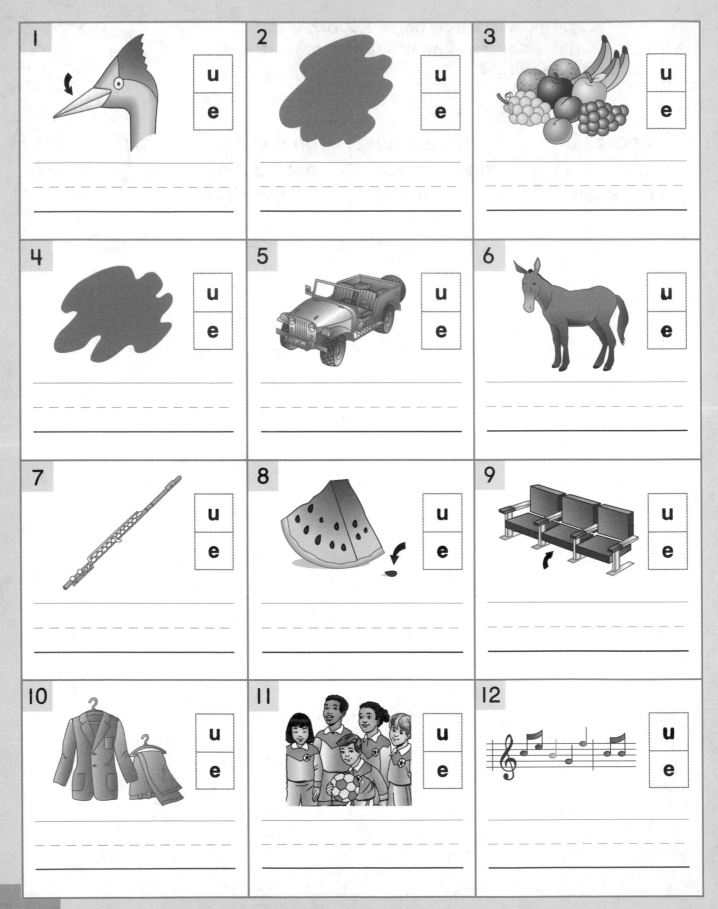

1 u / e

2 u / e

3 u / e

4 u / e

5 u / e

6 u / e

7 u / e

8 u / e

9 u / e

10 u / e

11 u / e

12 u / e

Spell and Write

Say and spell each word in the box. Then write each word under the long vowel sound in its name.

home
may
five
tune
tree
coat
fruit
eat
pie
make

1 Long **a**

2 Long **i**

3 Long **o**

4 Long **u**

5 Long **e**

**Spell and Write** Make a list of things to do as you sit under an apple tree.
Use two or more of your spelling words.

home	may	five	tune	tree
coat	fruit	eat	pie	make

Things To Do

hum a tune

Let's read and talk about a tree named General Sherman.

Did you ever hug a tree? Could you reach all the way around? Not if you hugged General Sherman! General Sherman is the name of a giant sequoia tree. It is the biggest giant sequoia in California. In fact, it is the biggest tree in the world. General Sherman's trunk is very, very wide. It would take about 25 children holding hands to make a circle around this huge tree.

How would you feel standing next to General Sherman in a forest of giant sequoia trees?

Check-Up Fill in the circle next to the word that names the picture.

1	
	○ van
	○ vane
	○ vine

2	
	○ glue
	○ clue
	○ glum

3	
	○ hat
	○ hay
	○ hand

4	
	○ said
	○ seed
	○ see

5	
	○ snail
	○ slow
	○ snow

6	
	○ tube
	○ tub
	○ tune

7	
	○ lack
	○ late
	○ lake

8	
	○ pine
	○ pie
	○ pane

9	
	○ bet
	○ beat
	○ boat

Underline all the words that have a long vowel sound.
Then circle **Yes** or **No** to answer each question.

10. Is a jeep the same as a jet?		Yes	No
11. Can a goat paint a gate?		Yes	No
12. Can a seal swim in the sea?		Yes	No
13. Is a peach a fruit?		Yes	No
14. Is a cape a big cap?		Yes	No
15. Can you hide a flute in a lime?		Yes	No
16. Is a dime the same as a vine?		Yes	No
17. Can you put ice cream in a cone?		Yes	No

LESSON 31: Assessing Long Vowels

CITY STREET

Honk—honk—honk!
Beep—beep—beep!
Hear the noise
Of city street.

Cars race fast,
Trucks bump past;
Creeping slow
The buses go.

Green turns red,
A sudden stop;
Up the hand
Of traffic cop.

Whistle shrill—
All is still;
Sudden hush—
The people rush.

Red turns green,
Then on again;
Cars race fast,
Trucks bump past.

Lois Lenski

Critical Thinking

How is the place where you live like this busy city?
How is it different?

Dear Family,

As your child progresses through this unit about cities, she or he will learn about the two sounds of **c** and **g** and about consonant blends. A **consonant blend** is two or three consonants sounded together in a word so that each letter is heard.

● Read the words below. Listen to the sounds of the letters that are underlined.

Apreciada Familia:

En esta unidad sobre las ciudades, su niño aprenderá los dos sonidos de las letras **c** y **g** y sobre combinación de sonidos de las consonantes. Una **combinación de sonido** se forma cuando dos o más consonantes están juntas pero cada una tiene su propio sonido al pronunciar la palabra.

● Lean las siguientes palabras. Escuchen el sonido de las letras subrayadas.

Soft c	Hard c
<u>c</u>ity	<u>c</u>ar

Soft g	Hard g
<u>g</u>ym	<u>g</u>o

Consonant Blends	
<u>pl</u>ay	re<u>nt</u>

● Read the poem "City Street" on the reverse side.

● Talk about the city scene.

● Point out the consonant sounds in these words from the poem: soft **c** (<u>c</u>ity, ra<u>c</u>e); hard **c** (<u>c</u>ars, <u>c</u>op); hard **g** (<u>g</u>o); consonant blends (ho<u>nk</u>, <u>str</u>eet, fa<u>st</u>, <u>tr</u>ucks, bump, <u>cr</u>eeping, <u>sl</u>ow, <u>gr</u>een, <u>st</u>op, ha<u>nd</u>, <u>tr</u>affic).

● Lean la poesía "City Street" en la página 67.

● Hablen de la escena en la ciudad.

● Señalen los sonidos de las consonantes en estas palabras de la poesía: **c** suave (<u>c</u>ity, ra<u>c</u>e); **c** fuerte (<u>c</u>ars, <u>c</u>op); **g** fuerte (<u>g</u>o); combinación de consonantes (ho<u>nk</u>, <u>str</u>eet, fa<u>st</u>, <u>tr</u>ucks, bump, <u>cr</u>eeping, <u>sl</u>ow, <u>gr</u>een, <u>st</u>op, ha<u>nd</u>, <u>tr</u>affic).

PROJECT

Make a city skyscraper with your child. Use index cards or rectangular pieces of paper for the bricks. When your child learns a new word with soft or hard **c** or **g** or with a consonant blend, have him or her write the word on a brick and add it to the building.

PROYECTO

Junto con el niño hagan un rascacielos. Use tarjetas 3X5 o pedazos de papel para los ladrillos. Cuando el niño aprenda una palabra nueva con sonidos suave o fuerte de la **c** o la **g**, o de combinación, pídale escribir la palabra en un ladrillo y pegarlo al edificio.

Helpful Hint

C usually has the soft sound when it is followed by **e, i,** or **y**.

City has the soft **c** sound. **Car** has the hard **c** sound. Say the name of each picture. Circle **Soft c** if the word has the soft **c** sound. Circle **Hard c** if it has the hard **c** sound.

1	2	3
city	car	race
Soft **c** Hard **c**	Soft **c** Hard **c**	Soft **c** Hard **c**

4	5	6
cone	rice	can
Soft **c** Hard **c**	Soft **c** Hard **c**	Soft **c** Hard **c**

7	8	9
dice	celery	cane
Soft **c** Hard **c**	Soft **c** Hard **c**	Soft **c** Hard **c**

10	11	12
pencil	cave	cube
Soft **c** Hard **c**	Soft **c** Hard **c**	Soft **c** Hard **c**

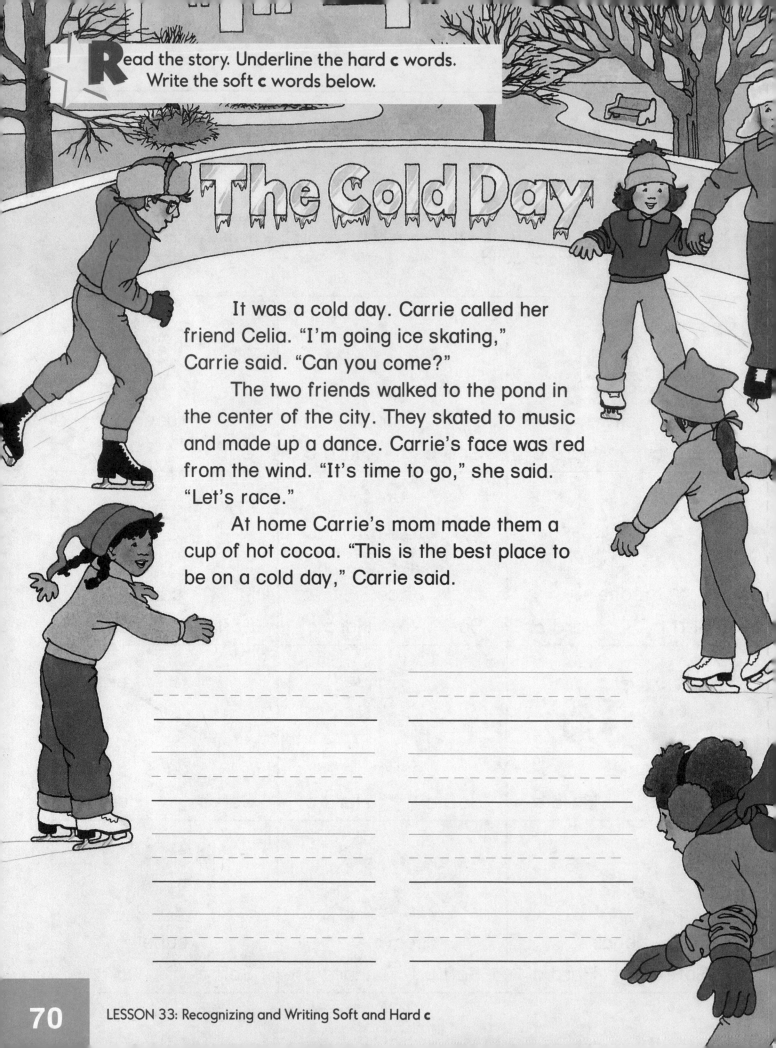

Read the story. Underline the hard **c** words. Write the soft **c** words below.

The Cold Day

It was a cold day. Carrie called her friend Celia. "I'm going ice skating," Carrie said. "Can you come?"

The two friends walked to the pond in the center of the city. They skated to music and made up a dance. Carrie's face was red from the wind. "It's time to go," she said. "Let's race."

At home Carrie's mom made them a cup of hot cocoa. "This is the best place to be on a cold day," Carrie said.

G usually has the soft sound when it is followed by **e, i,** or **y**.

Stage has the soft **g** sound. **Gate** has the hard **g** sound. Say the name of each picture. Circle **Soft g** if the word has the soft **g** sound. Circle **Hard g** if it has the hard **g** sound.

1
stage
Soft **g**   Hard **g**

2
gate
Soft **g**   Hard **g**

3
gem
Soft **g**   Hard **g**

4
goat
Soft **g**   Hard **g**

5
gym
Soft **g**   Hard **g**

6
bag
Soft **g**   Hard **g**

7
giant
Soft **g**   Hard **g**

8
giraffe
Soft **g**   Hard **g**

9
wagon
Soft **g**   Hard **g**

10
gum
Soft **g**   Hard **g**

11
gas
Soft **g**   Hard **g**

12
cage
Soft **g**   Hard **g**

Read the movie titles on the posters. Underline the hard **g** words. Write the soft **g** words.

Make a movie poster. Write the title of a make-believe movie and draw a picture to go with it. In the title, use one soft **g** word and one hard **g** word.

Complete each line of the poem by writing a word from the box.
Read the poem and circle all of the hard **c** and **g** words.

| laces | game | car | gym | page | space |

Cindy has a friend who came _____

To join her in a jumping _____ .

Vince and Cal who run in races _____

Always stop to tie their _____ .

Gail and Gene set up on stage _____

And take their turns to read a _____ .

Look at the smile on Cam's face _____

As she hops from space to _____ .

Curt calls up his pal Kim _____

To shoot some baskets at the _____ .

Now on his bike Miguel goes far. _____

When he grows up, he'll drive a _____ .

LESSON 35: Reviewing Soft and Hard **c** and **g**

73

Circle the words in each list that have the same c or g sound as the picture name.

1	2	3	4
Soft **c**	Hard **c**	Soft **g**	Hard **g**
nice	cane	bag	goal
can	place	magic	wagon
come	cold	giraffe	giant
dance	cup	goat	gem

Write **S** beside each word that has the sound of soft **c** or **g**. Write **H** beside each word that has the sound of hard **c** or **g**.

5	6	7	8
cup _____	center _____	page _____	gate _____

9	10	11	12
gull _____	face _____	ice _____	car _____

13	14	15	16
gym _____	cage _____	gas _____	cube _____

17	18	19	20
race _____	fence _____	game _____	gentle _____

74   LESSON 35: Assessing Soft and Hard **c** and **g**

A consonant blend is two or three consonants sounded together in a word so that each letter is heard.

Globe begins with the **l-blend gl**. Circle the **l-blend** that begins each picture name.

1 	gl pl sl	2	gl pl fl	3	sl pl bl
4	bl cl fl	5	cl fl sl	6	sl gl bl
7	bl cl gl	8	bl sl pl	9	fl cl pl
10	pl sl fl	11	bl cl gl	12	fl gl bl

Write a sentence about something you see on a city block. For example, "I see a bank with two big **cl**ocks."

LESSON 36: Recognizing l-blends

75

Read each picture name. Then write a word with the same phonogram. Begin the new word with an **l**-blend from the box.

bl	cl	fl	gl	pl	sl

1	2	3
dad	**s**ock	**h**am
_____	_____	_____

4	5	6
hay	**h**ide	**g**oat
_____	_____	_____

Circle and write the word that completes each sentence.

_____

7. I'm _____ to see you.   glide   glad

_____

8. Let's go _____ at the park.   play   clay

_____

9. It's just two _____ away.   clocks   blocks

_____

10. We can try the new _____.   slide   slam

Train begins with the **r**-blend **tr**. Say the name of each picture. Add an **r**-blend to the phonogram to write the picture name.

br	cr	dr	fr	gr	pr	tr

1

_____ain

2

_____um

3

_____ow

4

_____ick

5

_____een

6

_____ize

7

_____ame

8

_____ill

9

_____ee

10

_____ide

11

_____og

12

_____ab

Taking Off

Work with your classmates to make a train of **r**-blends. Write a word that begins with an **r**-blend on each boxcar.

train brain

LESSON 37: Recognizing and Writing **r**-blends

77

Read each picture name. Then write a word with the same phonogram. Begin the new word with an **r**-blend from the box.

br	cr	dr	fr	gr	pr	tr

1

hill

_____

2

bee

_____

3

team

_____

4

lake

_____

5

game

_____

6

cape

_____

Use a word from the box to complete each phrase.

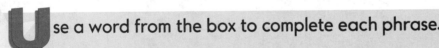

brake	cream	drill	frame	grape	tree

7. drink _____ juice

8. eat ice _____

9. step on the _____

10. get a picture _____

11. _____ a hole

12. plant a _____

Stamp begins with the **s**-blend **st**. Circle the pictures in each row whose names begin with the same **s**-blend as the first picture. Write the blend.

1 stamp

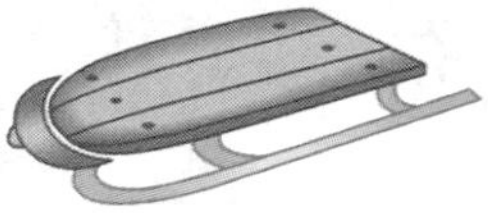

2 swing

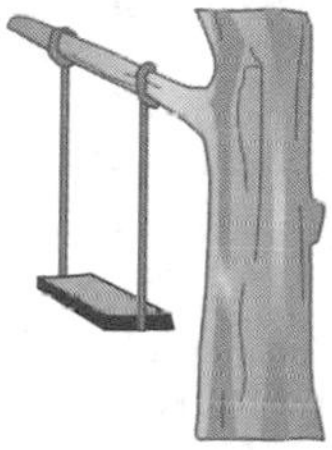

3 spill

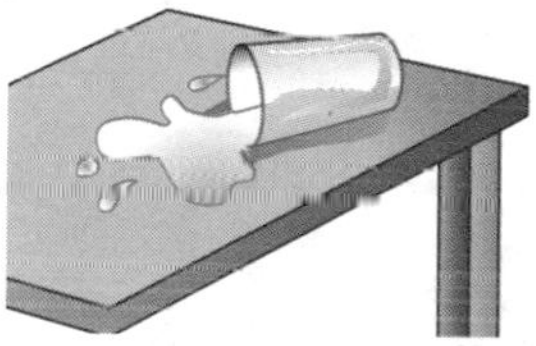

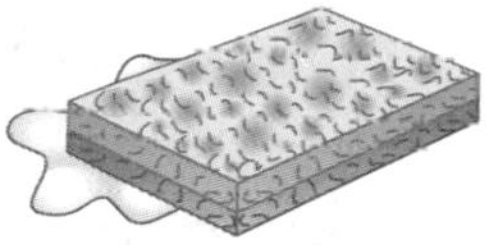

4 skate

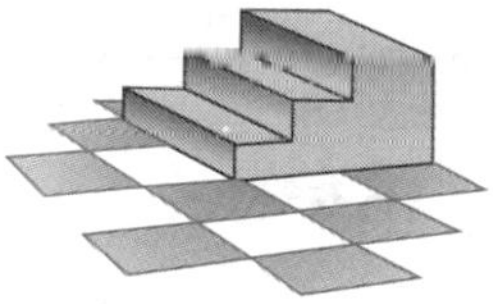

5 street

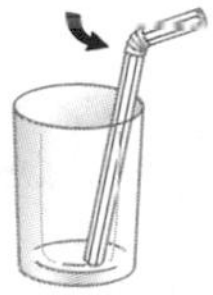

W rite a word with an **s**-blend to answer each question.

sc	sm	sn	squ	spr

1. What tells your weight and rhymes with **tale**? _____

2. What sound made by a mouse rhymes with **beak**? _____

3. What crawls in the grass and rhymes with **rake**? _____

4. What means "not large" and rhymes with **tall**? _____

5. What comes after winter and rhymes with **wing**? _____

C ircle and write an **s**-blend to complete the word in each sentence.

6. A big truck sweeps the city _____eet.   str   sw   sl

7. Brushes _____ub the street clean.   sc   scr   sn

8. The truck also _____ays water.   st   spr   spl

9. Watch out for the _____ash!   sl   sp   spl

Vest ends with the consonant blend **st**. Circle the blend that ends each picture name.

1	lf	2	ft	3	nt
	lt		lf		nd
	st		ld		nk

4	ft	5	nk	6	mp
	lt		nd		nt
	st		ld		st

7	lf	8	ft	9	nd
	nt		ld		mp
	mp		st		nk

10	st	11	lf	12	nd
	lt		lt		nk
	nt		ft		mp

Work with a partner. Write a list of words that end with the same blend as **nest**.

LESSON 39: Recognizing Final Blends

81

⭐ **W**rite a word with the same phonogram.

1 **v**est	**2** **b**ump	**3** **m**elt	**4** **l**ift
5 **c**old	**6** **w**ent	**7** **b**end	**8** **b**unk
9 **st**amp	**10** **dr**ink	**11** **st**and	**12** **tw**ist

⭐ **U**se a word from the box to complete each sentence.

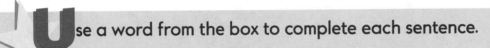

stand	went	best	drink

13. Last week Mom and I _____ to a street fair.

14. First we stopped at a fresh fruit _____.

15. Then we got grape juice to _____.

16. We had the _____ time together!

Look at the picture and read the word. Change the blend to write the word that names the picture.

1	2	3
pride	**gl**ue	**dr**ain

4	5	6
snow	**pl**ate	**sw**ing

7	8	9
smog	**sp**ill	**br**ing

10	11	12
scat	**gr**een	**cl**amp

Write the name of each picture in the puzzle. Then read the shaded letters down to find the answer to the question.

1		f	i	s	t

1   f i s t

2   ___ ___ ___ ___

3   ___ ___ ___ ___

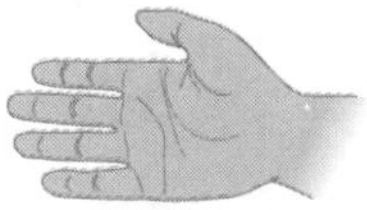

4   ___ ___ ___ ___

5   ___ ___ ___ ___

6   ___ ___ ___ ___

7   ___ ___ ___ ___ ___

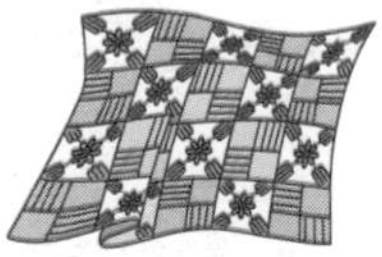

8   ___ ___ ___ ___

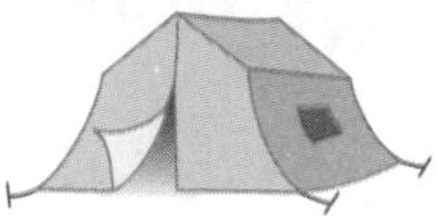

9   ___ ___ ___ ___

10   ___ ___ ___ ___

What are two consonants sounded together at the end of a word?

_____   _____

a _____   _____

Spell and Write

Say and spell each word in the box. Then write each word under the blend in its name.

| train |
| glue |
| jump |
| flag |
| space |
| green |
| help |
| stage |
| play |
| fast |
| from |
| street |

1 l-blend

2 r-blend

3 s-blend

4 Final Blend

Join the stage crew for a class play called "City Streets." Plan the scenery and the sound effects. Write what you will see and hear on the stage. Use two or more of your spelling words.

train	glue	jump	flag	space	green	
help	stage	play	fast	from		street

City STREETS

Scenery: What You Will See

_____

_____

_____

_____

_____

_____

_____

Sound Effects: What You Will Hear

_____

_____

_____

_____

_____

_____

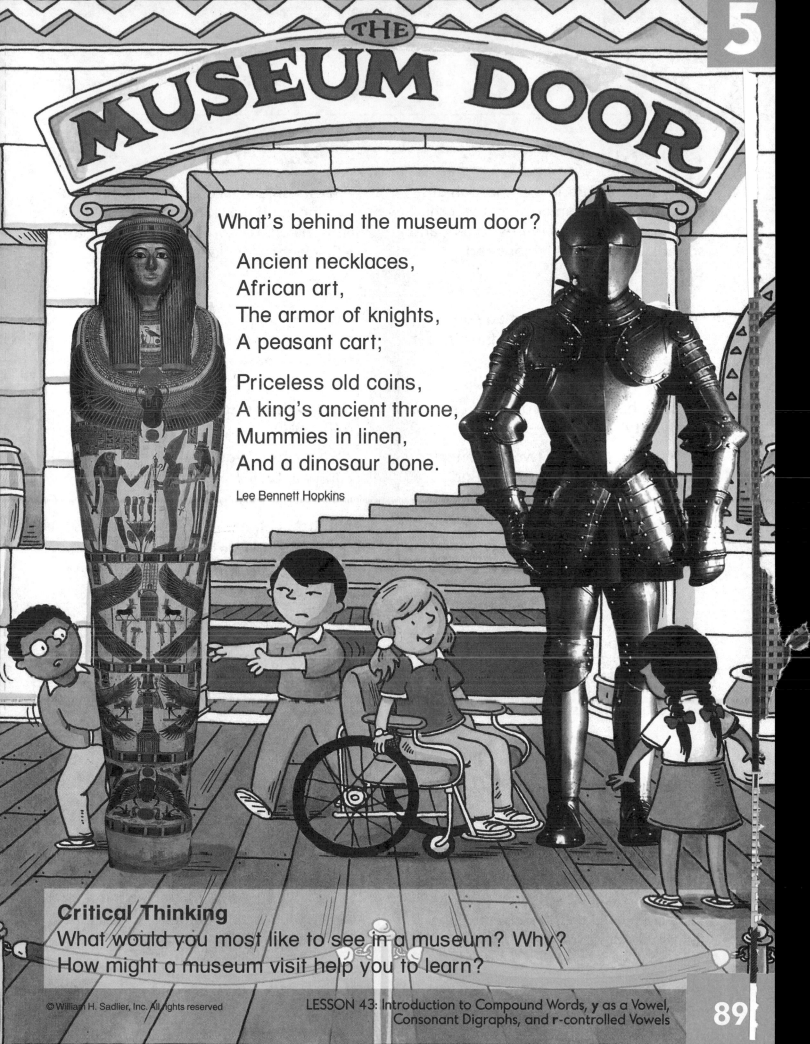

THE MUSEUM DOOR

What's behind the museum door?

Ancient necklaces,
African art,
The armor of knights,
A peasant cart;

Priceless old coins,
A king's ancient throne,
Mummies in linen,
And a dinosaur bone.

Lee Bennett Hopkins

Critical Thinking
What would you most like to see in a museum? Why?
How might a museum visit help you to learn?

LESSON 43: Introduction to Compound Words, y as a Vowel,
Consonant Digraphs, and r-controlled Vowels

Dear Family,

As your child progresses through this unit about going places, he or she will learn more about words, letters, and sounds. Read the definitions and examples together.

> **compound word:** word made up of two or more smaller words (**raincoat, baseball**)
>
> **words with y as a vowel:** words in which **y** has the sound of long **i** or long **e** (**fl**y, **cit**y)
>
> **consonant digraph:** two consonants together that stand for one sound (**ch**in, **tooth**)
>
> **words with ar, or, er, ir, ur:** words in which **r** gives the vowel a new sound (**b**ar**n, c**or**n, f**er**n, b**ir**d, t**ur**n**)

- Read the poem "The Museum Door" on the reverse side.

- Talk about museums or other interesting places you have visited.

Apreciada Familia:

En esta unidad, acerca de los paseos, su niño continuará aprendiendo sobre letras, palabras y sonidos. Juntos lean las definiciones y los ejemplos.

> **palabras compuestas:** aquellas formadas por dos o más palabras (**raincoat, baseball**).
>
> **y con sonido de vocal:** palabras en las que la **y** tiene el sonido largo de la **i** o la **e** (**fl**y, **cit**y).
>
> **consonantes digrafas:** dos consonantes juntas que producen un solo sonido (**ch**in, **tooth**).
>
> **palabras con ar, or, er, ir, ur:** palabras donde la letra **r** da a la vocal un nuevo sonido (**b**ar**n, c**or**n, f**er**n, b**ir**d, t**ur**n**).

- Lea la poesía, "The Museum Door" en la página 89.

- Hablen de los museos u otros lugares interesantes que hayan visitado.

PROJECT

Have your child make a map of an imaginary town that she or he would like to visit. Together make up place names for the map from new words your child learns. Help your child label the map. Then "stroll" around town together.

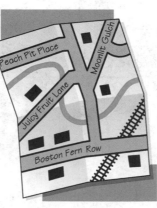

PROYECTO

Pida al niño dibujar el mapa de un pueblo imaginario el cual le gustaría visitar. Con las nuevas palabras busquen nombres para el mapa. Ayude al niño a rotular el mapa. Después caminen juntos por el pueblo.

A **compound word** is made up of two or more smaller words.

The compound word **starfish** is made up of **star** and **fish**. Combine a word from Box 1 with a word from Box 2 to name each picture. Write the compound words.

Box 1		
back	pea	rain
base	play	star
mail	pop	wind

Box 2		
ball	corn	nut
bow	fish	pack
box	mill	pen

1

2

3

4

5

6

7

8

9

LESSON 44: Recognizing and Writing Compound Words

Make compound words. Draw a line from each word in the first column to a word in the second column.

1	bean ●	● side	9	day ●	● cake
2	tea ●	● bag	10	pan ●	● weed
3	in ●	● coat	11	sea ●	● fruit
4	rain ●	● cup	12	grape ●	● dream
5	row ●	● self	13	suit ●	● case
6	sand ●	● flake	14	bee ●	● way
7	snow ●	● boat	15	week ●	● end
8	him ●	● box	16	run ●	● hive

Combine each word with a picture name and write the compound word.

17		20	
ant _____		cake _____	
18		21	
set _____		man _____	
19		22	
pine _____		tree _____	

If you could go **anywhere**, where would you go? Write about a place you would like to visit.

Helpful Hint

Every **syllable** has a vowel sound.
Words can have one, two, or more syllables.

The word **road** has one syllable. The word **wagon** has two syllables.
Say the name of each picture. Listen for the vowel sounds.
Write 1 or 2 for the number of vowel sounds you hear.

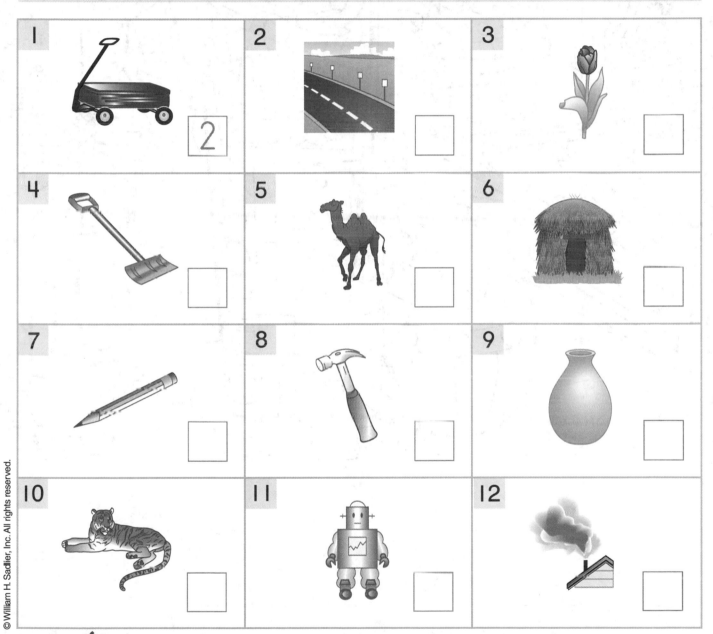

1. 2
2.
3.
4.
5.
6.
7.
8.
9.
10.
11.
12.

Taking Off

Say your name. Listen for vowel sounds. Do you have one or more
syllables in your first name? your last name?

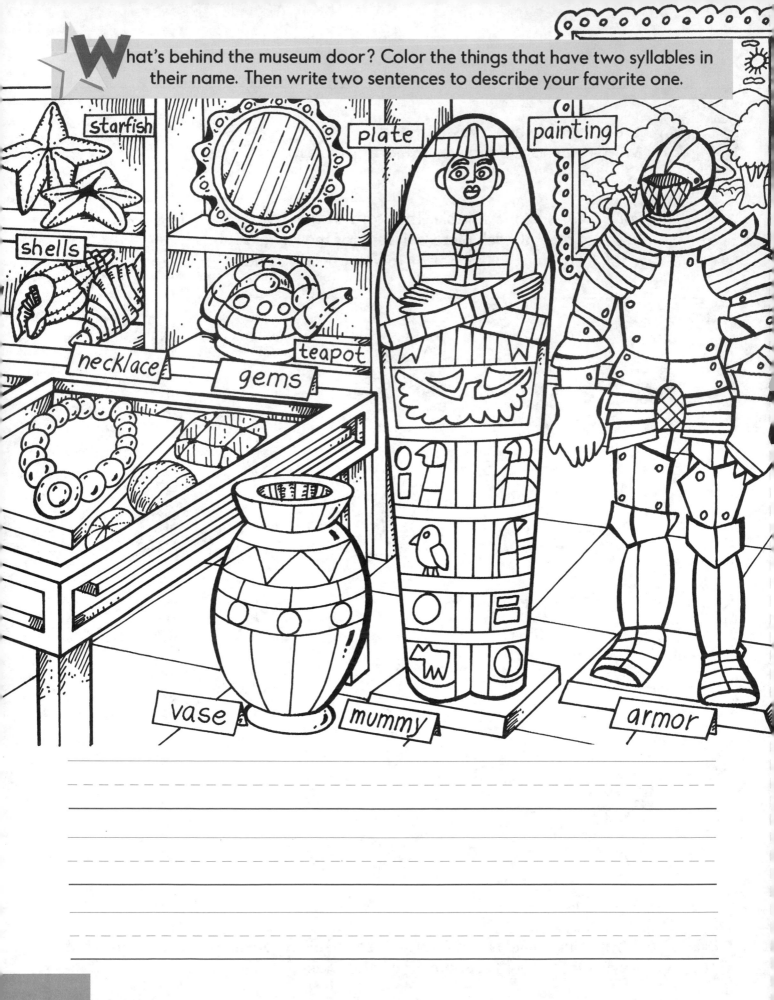

What's behind the museum door? Color the things that have two syllables in their name. Then write two sentences to describe your favorite one.

starfish

plate

painting

shells

necklace

gems

teapot

vase

mummy

armor

_____

_____

_____

_____

_____

Sometimes **y** has the sound of long **i**. Sometimes it has the sound of long **e**.

The **y** in **fly** has the long **i** sound. The **y** in **city** has the long **e** sound. Say the name of each picture. Circle **Long i** if the **y** has the long **i** sound. Circle **Long e** if it has the long **e** sound.

1 fly	2 city	3 penny
Long i Long e	Long i Long e	Long i Long e

4 cry	5 forty	6 sky
Long i Long e	Long i Long e	Long i Long e

7 bunny	8 candy	9 twenty
Long i Long e	Long i Long e	Long i Long e

10 dry	11 pony	12 daisy
Long i Long e	Long i Long e	Long i Long e

Visit the video library. Read the video titles. Underline the words in which **y** has the sound of long **i**. Write the words in which **y** has the sound of long **e**.

By Myself

A Chair for My Mother

Henny Penny

Home in the Sky

The Poppy Seed Cakes

Ty's One-Man Band

Ruby the Copycat

The Ugly Duckling

Why Can't I Fly?

_____   _____

_____   _____

_____   _____

_____   _____

Make up a title for a video or a book. Try to use one or two words with **y** as a vowel.

LESSON 46: Recognizing and Writing y as a Vowel

Write the compound word from the box that fits each clue.

| anthill | beanbag | beehive | rowboat | seaweed | snowflake |

1. This is a boat you row. _____

2. This is a hive for bees. _____

3. This is a hill made by ants. _____

4. This is a weed that grows in the sea. _____

5. This is a flake of snow. _____

6. This is a bag filled with beans. _____

Write **i** beside each word in which **y** has the long **i** sound. Write **e** beside each word in which **y** has the long **e** sound.

7 _____	8 _____	9 _____	10 _____
fly ____	city ____	try ____	daisy ____
11 _____	12 _____	13 _____	14 _____
candy ____	penny ____	dry ____	why ____

Make compound words. Draw a line from each word in the first column to a word in the second column. Write the new word.

ant •   • cake
tree •   • hill
pea •   • ball
base •   • top
pan •   • nut

pine •   • bow
in •   • end
tea •   • cone
rain •   • side
week •   • cup

1 _____

2 _____

3 _____

4 _____

5 _____

6 _____

7 _____

8 _____

9 _____

10 _____

Circle the words in which **y** has the same sound as the picture name.

11

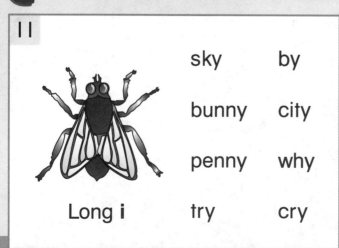

sky	by
bunny	city
penny	why

Long **i**   try   cry

12

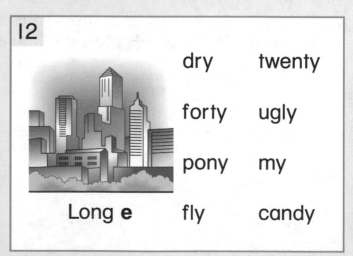

dry	twenty
forty	ugly
pony	my

Long **e**   fly   candy

LESSON 47: Assessing Compound Words and **y** as a Vowel

A **consonant digraph** is two consonants together that stand for one sound.

⭐ **T**humb begins with the consonant digraph **th**. Circle the consonant digraph that begins each picture name.

1		2		3	
	th sh wh		ch th sh		wh ch th
4		5		6	
	sh wh ch		th sh wh		ch th sh
7		8		9	
	wh sh th		sh wh ch		th ch wh
10		11		12	
	ch th sh		wh ch th		sh wh ch

Work with your classmates to list **thirteen** words that begin with consonant digraphs.

Circle and write the word that completes each sentence.

1. Do you know _____ the president lives?   where   what

2. _____ I give you a hint?   Shall   Chill

3. George Washington _____ the place.   chase   chose

4. But he didn't have a _____ to live there.   change   chance

5. It is painted _____.   white   wheat

6. I _____ it's a good place to visit.   thing   think

7. Let me _____ you Washington, D.C.   chow   show

Change the beginning digraph and write a rhyming word. Use **th, sh, wh,** or **ch**.

8 **ch**in	9 **ch**eep	10 **sh**op	11 **wh**ine
_____	_____	_____	_____

12 **sh**ip	13 **ch**eat	14 **wh**y	15 **th**ick
_____	_____	_____	_____

LESSON 48: Writing Initial Consonant Digraphs **th, sh, wh, ch**

Sock ends with the consonant digraph **ck**. Circle the consonant digraph that ends each picture name.

1	ck th sh	2	ch ck th	3	ch sh ck
4	th sh ch	5	ck th sh	6	ch ck th
7	ck ch sh	8	th ch sh	9	ck th sh

Circle the word that fits each clue.

10. This has wheels.	rock	truck
11. This is sandy.	beach	peach
12. This holds food.	duck	dish
13. This shows the time.	clock	click
14. This swims in the sea.	wish	fish
15. These show when you smile.	teeth	teach

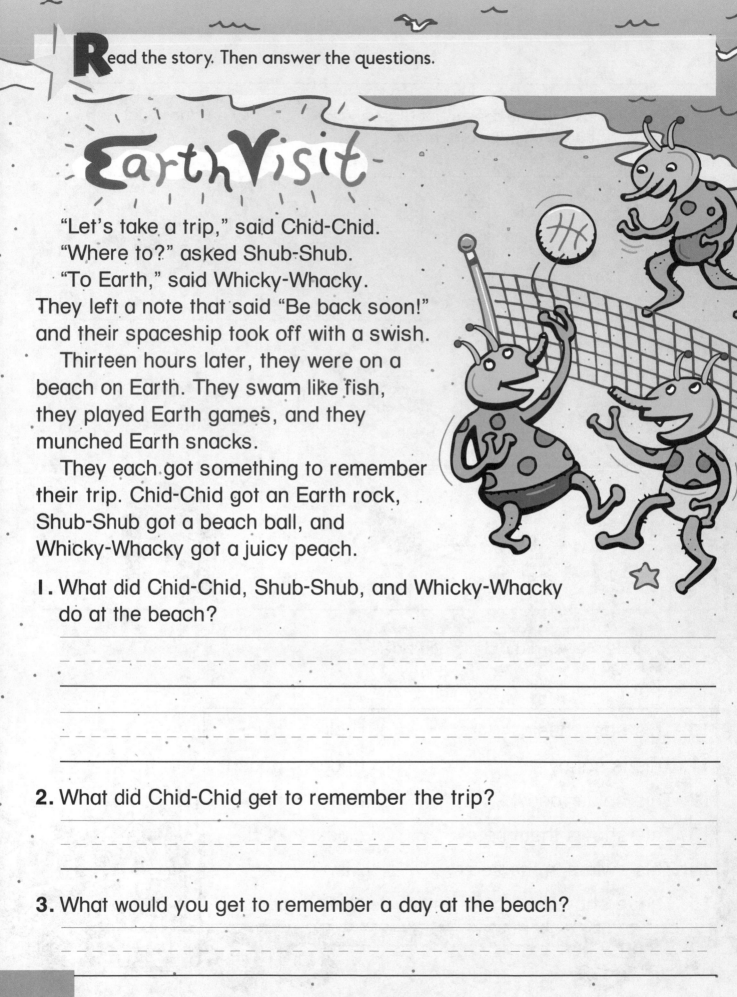

Earth Visit

"Let's take a trip," said Chid-Chid.
"Where to?" asked Shub-Shub.
"To Earth," said Whicky-Whacky.
They left a note that said "Be back soon!"
and their spaceship took off with a swish.

Thirteen hours later, they were on a
beach on Earth. They swam like fish,
they played Earth games, and they
munched Earth snacks.

They each got something to remember
their trip. Chid-Chid got an Earth rock,
Shub-Shub got a beach ball, and
Whicky-Whacky got a juicy peach.

1. What did Chid-Chid, Shub-Shub, and Whicky-Whacky
   do at the beach?

_____

- -

_____

- -

_____

2. What did Chid-Chid get to remember the trip?

_____

- -

_____

3. What would you get to remember a day at the beach?

_____

- -

_____

Knee begins with the consonant digraph **kn**. Find the name of each picture. Write the word.

knee   knight   knock   knot   knit   knife

1	2	3
_____	_____	_____

4	5	6
_____	_____	_____

Fill in the circle next to the word that completes the sentence. Write the word in the sentence.

7. I _____ a shop that sells all kinds of things.

○ know
○ knee

8. There is a _____ in armor at the door.

○ knife
○ knight

9. Just _____ and you can go inside.

○ knit
○ knock

10. You'll find brass _____ for your door.

○ knobs
○ knots

Wrist begins with the consonant digraph **wr**. Circle and write the word that names each picture.

1	rip	2	which	3	whip
	wrist		reach		wrap
	wish		wrench		ripe

4	write	5	read	6	rent
	white		wreath		went
	wheat		with		wren

Write a **wr**-word from above to complete each sentence.

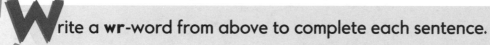

7. You _____ a letter.

8. You _____ a gift.

9. You hang a _____ on a door.

10. You use a _____ to fix things.

11. You wear a watch on your _____.

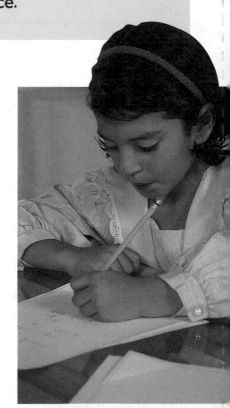

LESSON 50: Recognizing and Writing Consonant Digraph **wr**

Spell and Write Say and spell each word in the box. Then write each word under the digraph in its name. Circle the digraph in each word.

Word list
thorn
truck
chose
wrote
peach
why
knee
show
black
wash
both
what

1 th

2 sh

3 wh

4 ch

5 ck

6 kn

7 wr

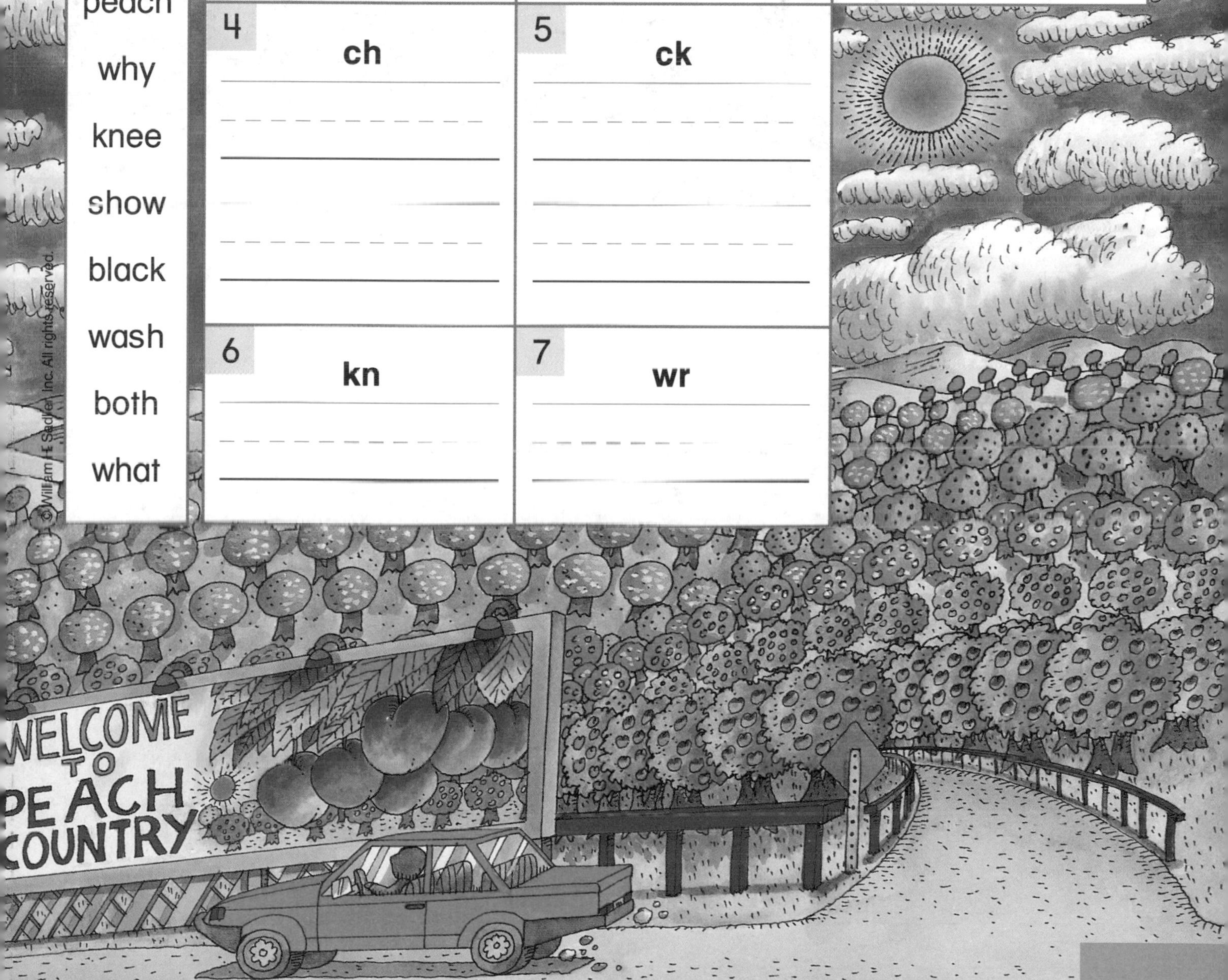

Be a tour guide. Welcome a visitor to your favorite place and tell about it. Write what you would say. Use one or more of your spelling words.

thorn	truck	chose	wrote	peach	why
knee	show	black	wash	both	what

Welcome to

Look at the picture clues. Write the words in the puzzle.

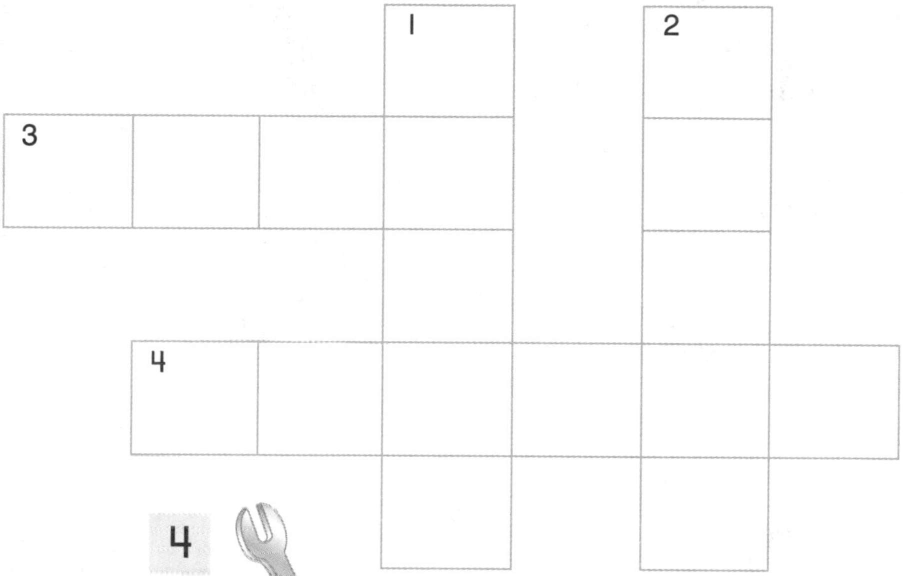

DOWN ⬇

1

2

ACROSS ➡

3

4

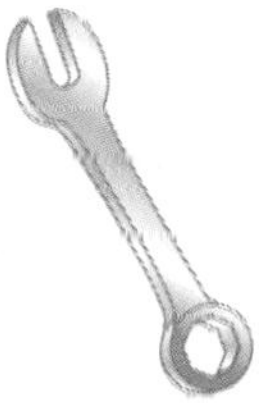

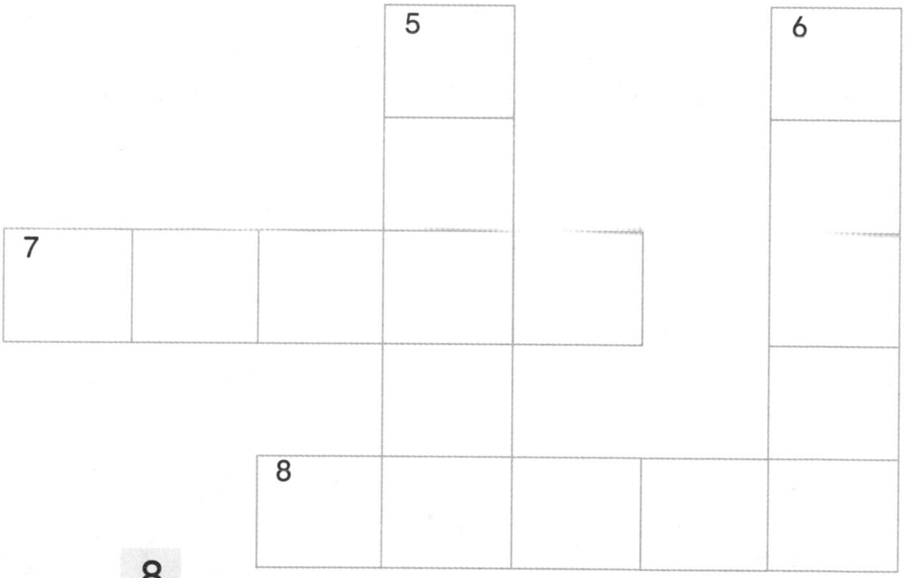

DOWN ⬇

5

6

ACROSS ➡

7

8

LESSON 52: Reviewing Consonant Digraphs

107

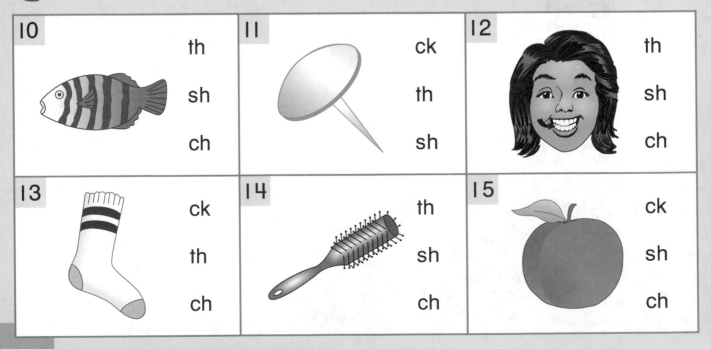

Check-Up Circle the consonant digraph that **begins** each picture name.

1 th sh wh	**2** wr ch wh	**3** th kn wr
4 wr sh wh	**5** sh kn ch	**6** sh th ch
7 sh wh ch	**8** th kn wh	**9** wr sh wh

Circle the consonant digraph that **ends** each picture name.

10 th sh ch	**11** ck th sh	**12** th sh ch
13 ck th ch	**14** th sh ch	**15** ck sh ch

LESSON 52: Assessing Consonant Digraphs

An **r** after a vowel gives the vowel a new sound.

Barn has the **ar** sound. Circle and write the word that names each picture.

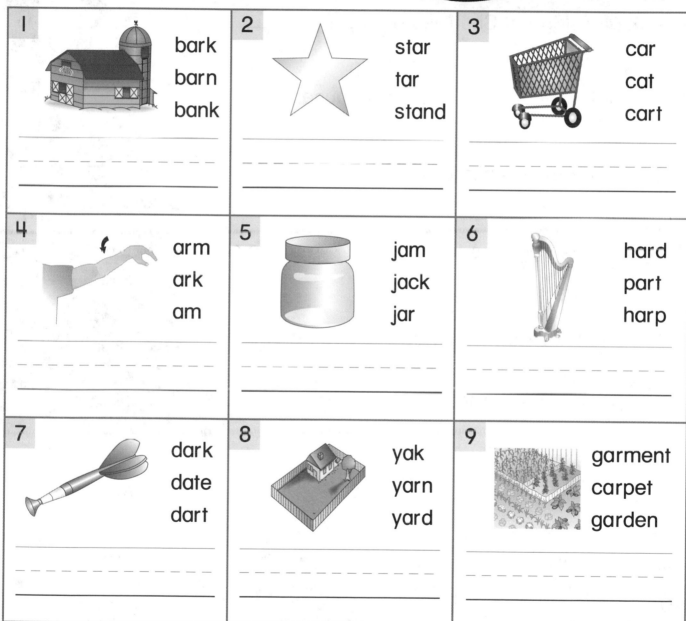

1	bark barn bank	2	star tar stand	3	car cat cart
4	arm ark am	5	jam jack jar	6	hard part harp
7	dark date dart	8	yak yarn yard	9	garment carpet garden

Talking Off

Write about a visit to a farm. Use some of these words in your sentences: **barn, dark, car, yard, garden.**

Use a word from the box to complete each sentence.

| far | dark | farm | hard | bark | barn |

_____

1. Is it _____ to milk a cow?

_____

2. Ask Mrs. Martin! She lives on a _____.

_____

3. It is not _____ from my house.

_____

4. There are many animals in the _____.

_____

5. Sparky the dog likes to _____ at the cows.

_____

6. Sometimes I visit until it gets _____.

Write a rhyming word.

7 harm	8 star	9 yard
_____	_____	_____
10 lark	11 yarn	12 dart
_____	_____	_____

Corn has the **or** sound. Find the name of each picture. Write the word.

acorn	cord	core	cork	corn	fork
forty	horn	horse	porch	thorn	torch

1 _____

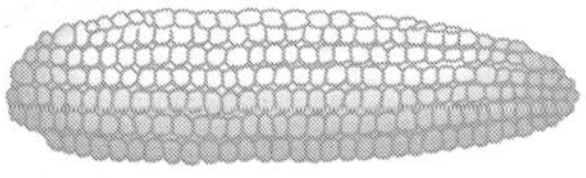

2 _____

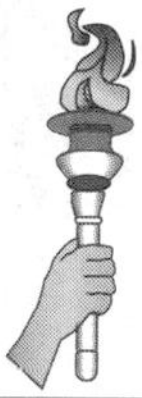

3 _____

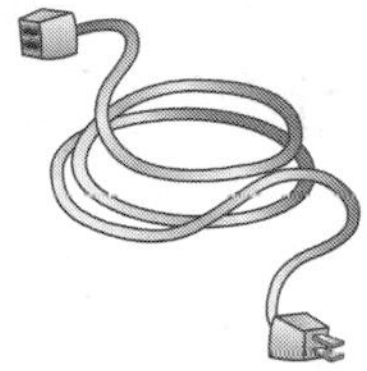

4 _____

5 _____

6 _____

7 _____

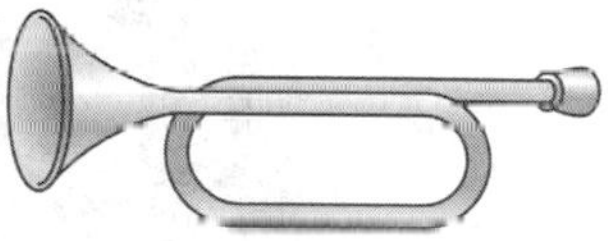

8 _____

9 _____

10 _____

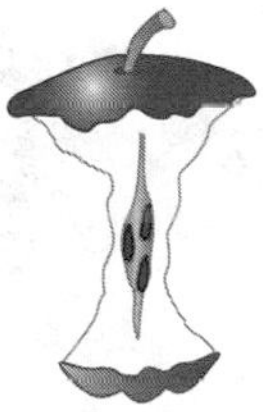

11 _____

12 _____

Draw a line from each word in the first column to a rhyming word in the second column.

1	park ●	● tar	9	farm ●	● worn
2	scar ●	● porch	10	form ●	● charm
3	sore ●	● spark	11	born ●	● yarn
4	torch ●	● more	12	barn ●	● storm
5	dark ●	● thorn	13	start ●	● mark
6	arm ●	● shore	14	pork ●	● stork
7	score ●	● harm	15	short ●	● smart
8	torn ●	● bark	16	shark ●	● sport

Circle all the **ar**-words. Underline all the **or**-words. Then circle **Yes** or **No** to answer each question.

17. Can a park path be short?	Yes	No
18. Can a horse play a harp?	Yes	No
19. Can you buy a scarf in a store?	Yes	No
20. Is a fork the same as a torch?	Yes	No
21. Can a shark throw darts?	Yes	No
22. Is an acorn made of yarn?	Yes	No
23. Can a stork play cards?	Yes	No
24. Can a dog bark and snarl?	Yes	No
25. Does corn have thorns?	Yes	No
26. Can you read a story in the morning?	Yes	No

The **er** in **fern,** the **ir** in **bird,** and the **ur** in **turtle** make the same sound. Sort the words. Write the **er**-words under **fern,** the **ir**-words under **bird,** and the **ur**-words under **purse.**

burn	chirp	clerk	curb	dirt	first
girl	her	herd	nurse	perch	serve
surf	term	third	thirty	turkey	turn

1

fern

2

bird

3

purse

Talking Off

Write a silly sentence with an **er**-word, an **ir**-word, and a **ur**-word. For example, "At the **turkey** farm, I saw **thirty birds** on one **perch.**"

1. Let's go to the _____.

   ○ circus
   ○ curve

2. Please _____ or we'll be late.

   ○ furry
   ○ hurry

3. Mom will be _____ in line.

   ○ fir
   ○ first

4. I'll stand next to _____.

   ○ her
   ○ hurt

5. You can be _____.

   ○ third
   ○ thirst

6. See the big cat with the striped _____.

   ○ fern
   ○ fur

7. Watch the cat _____ through the hoop.

   ○ squirt
   ○ burst

8. Can you hear the big cat _____?

   ○ chirp
   ○ purr

9. Watch the trainer _____ his whip.

   ○ stir
   ○ twirl

10. When can I have a _____?

    ○ turn
    ○ term

Remember

A **nursery** is a place where plants are grown and sold. Look at the picture of the nursery. Then follow the directions below.

Directions

1. Circle the name of the nursery.
2. Make an X on the clerk.
3. Color the bird blue and yellow.
4. Color the bird's perch brown.
5. Draw a box around the turtle.
6. Color the turnip tops green.
7. Color the fir trees blue.
8. Draw some ferns in the dirt.
9. Color the girl's skirt purple.
10. Color the boy's T-shirt red.
11. Draw a star on the purse.
12. Draw a furry kitten anywhere.

Write a story about visiting a nursery. Circle the **er**-words, **ir**-words, and **ur**-words that you use. Use some of the words in the box.

| birch | bird | chirp | clerk | dirt | fern |
| first | nursery | perch | purple | serve | turn |

Spell and Write Say and spell each word in the box. Then write each word under the correct heading.

clerk

start

purse

store

first

her

before

turn

far

horse

girl

herd

1 **er**-words

ir-words

ur-words

2 **or**-words

3 **ar**-words

PHOTOS

Spell and Write

Write a letter to a friend. Tell about a trip that you have taken or would like to take. Use one or more of your spelling words.

clerk	start	purse	store
first	her	before	turn
far	horse	girl	herd

Dear _____,

You'll never guess where
I went!

Your friend,

Look and Learn

Let's read and talk about the Statue of Liberty.

Meet Miss Liberty. That's what some people call this statue. She stands on an island in New York harbor and greets people who come to the United States. Miss Liberty is over 100 years old. She was a gift to us from the people of France. She's 152 feet high on a base that's 150 feet high. She holds the torch of freedom above her head.

Why do you think Miss Liberty holds the torch of freedom above her head?

 **Check-Up** Fill in the circle next to the word that names the picture.

1	2	3
○ car ○ core ○ curb	○ bark ○ bird ○ bore	○ fork ○ far ○ fern

4	5	6
○ barn ○ burn ○ born	○ harp ○ horn ○ horse	○ pork ○ perch ○ purse

Write the word from the box that fits each clue.

fork	her	large	perch	shirt	turn

7. This is where birds sit. _____

8. This goes with a knife. _____

9. This means the same as **big**. _____

10. This is something you put on. _____

11. This means the same as **spin**. _____

12. This is what you can call a girl. _____

120   LESSON 58: Assessing **r**-controlled Vowels

WHAT IS BROWN?

Brown is the color of
  a country road
Back of a turtle
Back of a toad.
Brown is cinnamon
And morning toast
And the good smell of
The Sunday roast.
Brown is the color of work
And the sound of a river,
Brown is bronze and a bow
And a quiver.
Brown is the house
On the edge of town
Where wind is tearing
The shingles down.

Mary O'Neill

Critical Thinking
How would you color the things outside your home?
What does your favorite color make you think of?

Dear Family,

As your child progresses through this unit about colors, she or he will review vowel pairs and learn about vowel digraphs and diphthongs. Read the definitions and examples together.

> **vowel pair:** two vowels that come together to make one long vowel sound (gr**ee**n, gr**ay**)
>
> **vowel digraph:** two vowels that come together to make a long sound, a short sound, or a special sound (br**ea**d, h**oo**k, p**au**se, l**aw**n)
>
> **diphthong:** two letters blended together to make one vowel sound (br**ow**n, h**ou**se, c**oi**n, t**oy**)

- Read the poem "What Is Brown?" on the reverse side.
- Look for words that have vowel pairs, vowel digraphs, or diphthongs. (br**ow**n, r**oa**d, t**oa**d, t**oa**st, g**oo**d, Sund**ay**, r**oa**st, s**ou**nd, b**ow**, h**ou**se, t**ow**n, d**ow**n)
- Talk about other colors that you see every day.

PROJECT

Ask your child to draw a rainbow on a large sheet of paper. When your child learns a word that has a vowel pair, vowel digraph, or diphthong, suggest that he or she write it under the rainbow. Your child can practice reading the words and using them in sentences.

brown gray
new hook
cloud boy

Apreciada Familia:

En esta unidad, sobre los colores, su niño aprenderá vocales apareadas, vocales digrafas y los diptongos. Lea las definiciones y los ejemplos con su niño.

> **vocales apareadas:** dos vocales que al unirse producen un sonido largo (gr**ee**n, gr**ay**).
>
> **vocales digrafas:** dos vocales que al unirse producen un sonido largo, corto o especial (br**ea**d, h**oo**k, p**au**se, l**aw**n).
>
> **diptongos:** dos letras que al unirse producen un sonido (br**ow**n, h**ou**se, c**oi**n, t**oy**).

- Lea la poesía, "What Is Brown?" en la página 121.
- Busquen palabras que tengan pares de vocales, vocales digrafas y diptongos (br**ow**n, r**oa**d, t**oa**d, t**oa**st, g**oo**d, Sund**ay**, r**oa**st, s**ou**nd, b**ow**, h**ou**se, t**ow**n, d**ow**n).
- Hablen de los colores que ven todos los días.

PROYECTO

Pida al niño dibujar un arco iris en un papel grande. Cuando el niño aprenda palabras con vocales apareadas, digrafas o diptongos puede escribirlas debajo del arco iris. Luego puede practicar leyendo y usando las palabras en oraciones.

Remember! If there are two vowels in a one-syllable word, the first vowel is usually long and the second vowel is silent. These two vowels together are a **vowel pair**.

The vowel pairs **ai** and **ay** stand for the long **a** sound in **rain** and **hay**. Circle the long **a** word that names each picture. Write the word.

1. run / ran / rain

2. ham / hail / hay

3. mail / mall / mill

4. jail / jay / jam

5. chat / chin / chain

6. sail / snail / snake

7. pay / pain / pail

8. sell / sail / sill

9. tree / tray / try

Taking Off

What would you p**ai**nt on a r**ai**ny d**ay**? Write about it.

Use a word from the box to complete each sentence. Then read the story.

| day | Gail | hay | sail | trail |

The Silver Train

A train ride is fun on a sunny

_____

_____. Look out and you'll see a farm

_____

with bales of golden _____. There's a

_____

lake and a boat with a white _____. And

_____

there's my friend _____! She's riding a

_____

black horse along a _____.

What else might you see on a train ride? Write about it.

_____

_____

_____

_____

LESSON 60: Writing Vowel Pairs **ai** and **ay**

The vowel pairs **ea** and **ee** stand for the long **e** sound in **seat** and **jeep**. Find the name of each picture. Write the word.

bee	feet	jeep	leaf	
seal	seat	seed	team	

1

2

3

4

5

6

7

8

Write a rhyming word.

9	10	11	12
beat	sleep	dream	weed

Write each word under the correct heading.

| peep | stream | sheep | creek | tweet |
| seal | beaver | tree | squeal |

1 Names of Animals	2 Sounds of Animals	3 Homes of Animals

Circle and write the word that completes each sentence.

4. Beavers have sharp _____.   beaks   teeth

5. They have webbed _____.   seats   feet

6. They live in creeks and _____.   streams   streets

7. They make dams from _____.   beans   trees

8. They _____ grass and bark.   eat   sleep

LESSON 61: Writing Vowel Pairs **ea** and **ee**

Follow the directions to make new words and find the answer to each riddle.

What are hard and white and sometimes fall out?

START with: **gray**

1. Change the **gr** to **tr**.   tray

2. Change the **ay** to **ee**.

3. Change the **tr** to **t**.

4. Add **th** to the end.

What is gold or silver, short or long, weak or strong?

START with: **real**

5. Change the **r** to **m**.

6. Change the **ea** to **ai**.

7. Change the **l** to **n**.

8. Change the **m** to **ch**.

LESSON 62: Reviewing Vowel pairs **ai, ay, ea, ee**

Complete each line of the poem by writing a word from the box.
Read the poem, and underline all the **ai** words and **ay** words.
Circle all the **ea** words and **ee** words.

| bee | keep | play | peak | tails | trail |

GREEN GRASS

Green is the grass under the snail. _____

Get down close to see its _____.

Black is the jeep making a squeak. _____

Will it ever reach the _____?

White is the seed I planted so deep. _____

Here is a pumpkin you can _____.

Blue is the jay in the old oak tree. _____

Out of a hive comes a buzzing _____.

Silver is the train on steel rails. _____

Dogs run by and wag their _____.

Yellow is the sun that shines today. _____

Let's go out. It's time to _____.

LESSON 62: Reviewing Vowel Pairs **ai, ay, ea, ee**

The vowel pairs **oa, ow,** and **oe** stand for the long **o** sound in **boat, snow,** and **hoe**. Circle the long **o** word that names each picture.

1		2		3	
	beat **boat** bat		**snow** snail snore		home hay **hoe**
4		5		6	
	sole seep **soap**		tea **toe** tone		ray **row** rope

The underlined word in each sentence does not make sense. Write a long **o** word from the box that would make sense.

blow	coat	doe	road	snow

7. Put on your <u>cute</u> and hat. _____

8. Feel the cold wind <u>blue</u>. _____

9. Look at the tracks in the white <u>snail</u>. _____

10. The tracks go across the <u>raid</u>. _____

11. It's a mother <u>day</u> with her baby. _____

The vowel pairs **ui** and **ue** stand for the long **u** sound in **fruit** and **glue**. The vowel pair **ie** stands for the long **i** sound in **tie**. Circle the word that names each picture.

1	fry / fruit / free	2	glue / glee / glow	3	tea / toe / tie
4	black / blue / blow	5	pea / pay / pie	6	seat / suit / sue

Write the word from the box that fits each clue.

fruit	glue	tie	pie	juice

7. This can come from an orange. _____

8. This can grow on a tree. _____

9. This can make things stick. _____

10. This is something you bake. _____

11. This is something you wear. _____

Write the name of each picture. Then find and circle the words in the puzzle. Look across and down.

1		2	
	_____		_____
3	_____	**4**	_____
5	_____	**6**	_____
7	_____	**8**	_____

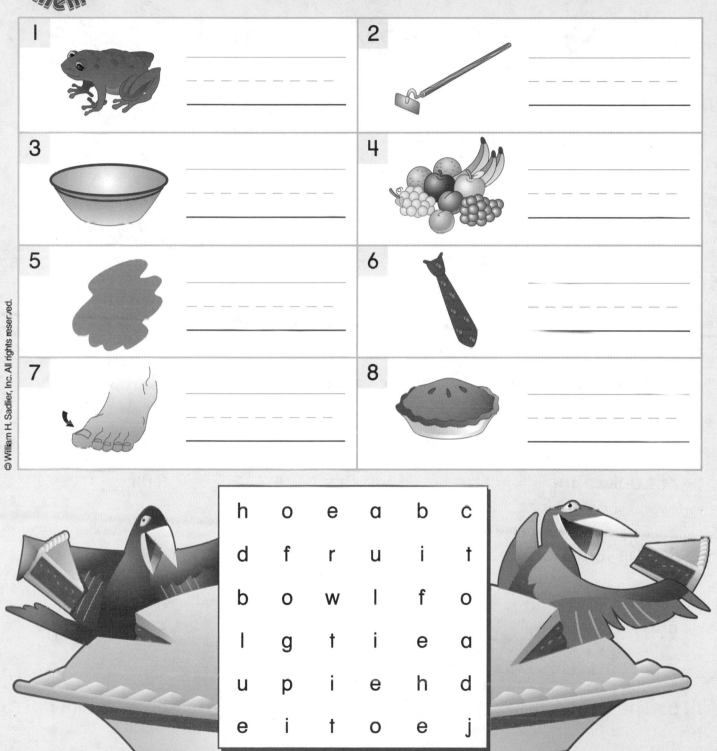

h	o	e	a	b	c
d	f	r	u	i	t
b	o	w	l	f	o
l	g	t	i	e	a
u	p	i	e	h	d
e	i	t	o	e	j

Check-Up Color the box that contains the vowel pair in each picture name. Write the word.

1		2		3	
	ui / oa / ie		ow / ay / ue		ea / oe / ui

4		5		6	
	ee / ui / ai		ea / ue / ie		ee / ow / ay

Circle and write the word that completes each sentence.

7. Look at the _____ in this bowl.   fruit   freeze

8. The lemons are _____.   yelling   yellow

9. The limes are a pretty shade of _____.   green   grain

10. The plums are _____.   blue   blow

11. Do you know the color of the _____?   poach   peach

132   LESSON 64: Assessing Vowel Pairs

A **vowel digraph** is two letters together that stand for one vowel sound. The vowel sound can be long or short, or the vowel digraph can have a sound of its own.

The vowel digraph **ea** can stand for the short **e** sound in **bread**. Circle and write the word that names each picture. Color the pictures in which **ea** has the short **e** sound.

1	2	3
bread bride	mail meat	heat head

4	5	6
feather farther	loaf leaf	spread sprain

7	8	9
pies peas	meeting measure	seal seam

Welcome to Rainbow Land

Jean grabbed a leather coat. Joan grabbed a sweater. They went out after breakfast. Something was wrong! The sky was pink instead of blue. The leaves on the trees were silver.

"I'm not ready for this," Jean said. "I'm going back to bed."

"Wait," said Joan. "There's a trail of yellow beans. Let's see where they lead."

Jean and Joan followed the trail to a peach meadow. Just ahead they saw a green gingerbread house.

What happened next? Write about it. Try to use some of these words: **feather, heavy, spread, thread, weather**.

The vowel digraph **oo** can stand for the vowel sound in **moon** or the vowel sound in **hook**. Write the name of each picture.

1

2

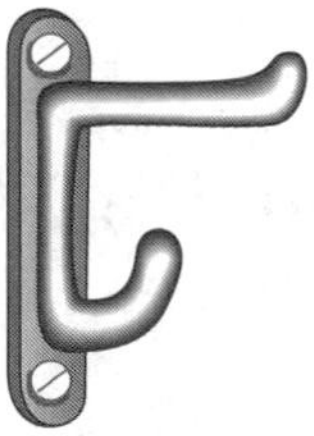

3

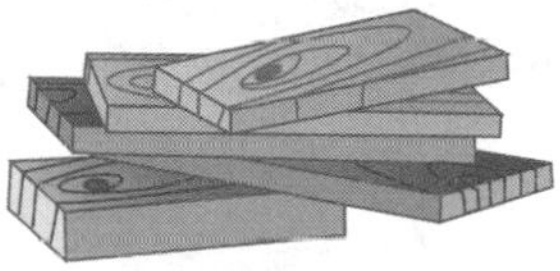

4

5

6

7

8

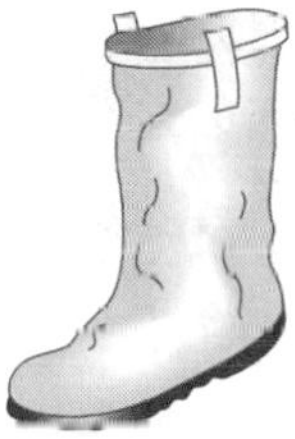

9

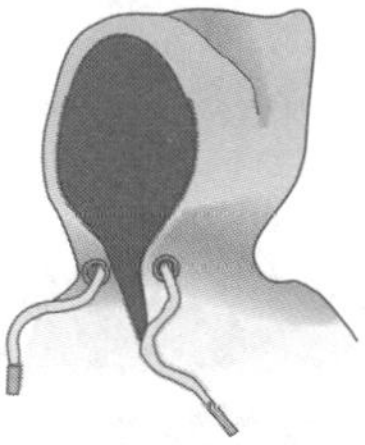

10

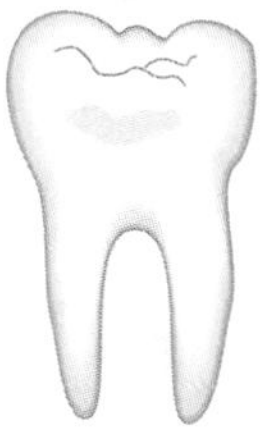

11

12

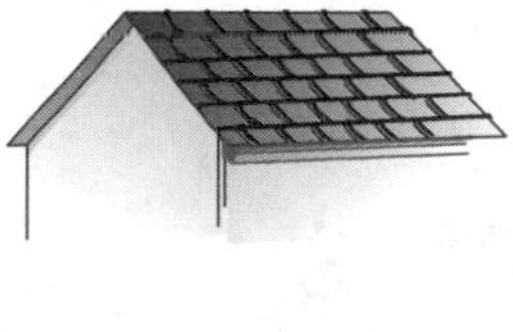

LESSON 66: Recognizing and Writing Vowel Digraph **oo**

135

Write an **oo** word to answer each question.

1. What tool for eating rhymes with **moon**? _____

2. What kind of stream rhymes with **hook**? _____

3. What part of a horse rhymes with **roof**? _____

4. What home for animals rhymes with **moo**? _____

5. What part of a coat rhymes with **good**? _____

6. What tool for sweeping rhymes with **loom**? _____

Circle and write the word that completes each sentence.

_____

7. A _____ is a kind of seat.   spool   stool

_____

8. I made a stool from _____.   wool   wood

_____

9. I sanded the stool to make it _____.   soon   smooth

_____

10. I painted it the color of my _____.   room   root

The vowel digraphs **au** and **aw** can stand for the vowel sound in **launch** and **paw**. Find the name of each picture. Write the word. In the last box, write the word that is not used and draw a picture to go with it.

| August | claw | crawl | faucet | hawk | launch |
| laundry | lawn | paw | sausage | saw | straw |

1.

2.

3.

4.

5.

6.

7.

8.

9.

10.

11.

12.

LESSON 67: Recognizing and Writing Vowel Digraphs **au** and **aw**

137

Circle the words that have the same vowel sound as **launch** and **paw**.

sauce	clue	haul	play
fault	yawn	head	cause
pause	thread	shawl	breath
jaw	fawn	spread	draw

Fill in the circle next to the word that completes the sentence. Write the word in the sentence.

1. Last _____ I stayed with Aunt Paula.

   ○ auto
   ○ autumn

2. We woke up at _____ .

   ○ drawn
   ○ dawn

3. We looked out and saw a brown _____ .

   ○ hawk
   ○ law

4. It had a hooked beak and sharp _____ .

   ○ thaws
   ○ claws

5. We also saw a spotted _____ .

   ○ fawn
   ○ yawn

6. It ran across Aunt Paula's _____ .

   ○ lawn
   ○ jaw

7. It _____ to look back at us.

   ○ caused
   ○ paused

Write about something you like to do in the autumn.

LESSON 67: Recognizing and Writing Vowel Digraphs **au** and **aw**

Write the name of each picture in the puzzle. Then read the shaded letters down to find the answer to the question.

1

2

3

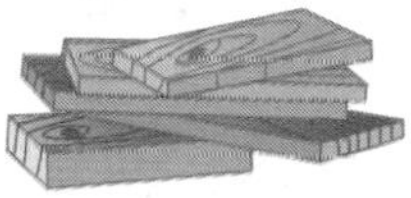

4

5

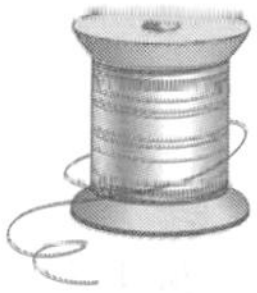

6

7

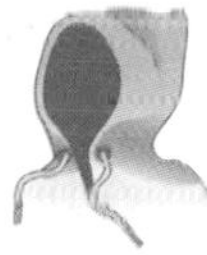

8

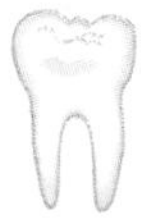

9

10

What is gray or white and hard to catch?

a _____ _____

Color the box that contains the vowel digraph in each picture name. Write the word.

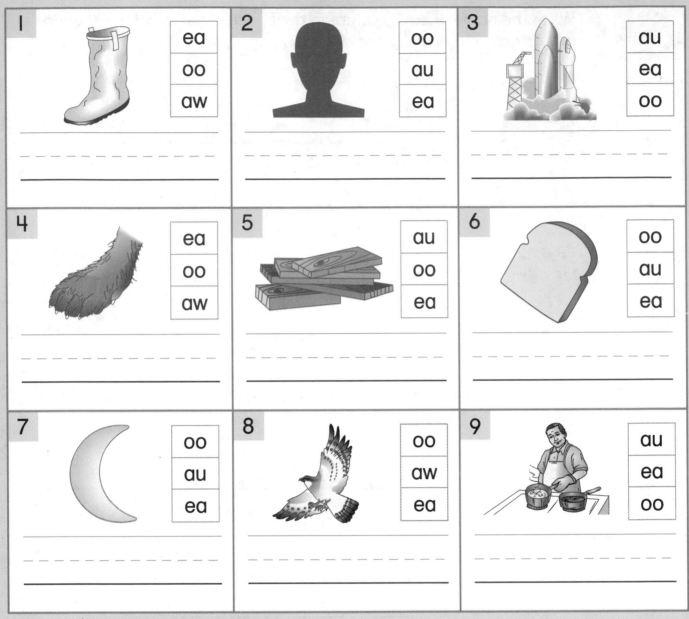

1 ea / oo / aw

2 oo / au / ea

3 au / ea / oo

4 ea / oo / aw

5 au / oo / ea

6 oo / au / ea

7 oo / au / ea

8 oo / aw / ea

9 au / ea / oo

Circle the word that fits each clue.

10. You use this to eat.   stood   spoon   soon

11. Water comes out of this.   faucet   fault   pause

12. You do this on paper.   thaw   straw   draw

13. You can read this.   book   hood   hoof

14. You can wear this.   instead   sweater   thread

A **diphthong** is two letters blended together that stand for one vowel sound.

The diphthong **ow** can stand for the vowel sound in **brown**. Say the name of each picture. Circle **Diphthong** if the word has the vowel sound in **brown**. Circle **Long o** if the word has the vowel sound in **snow**.

1 brown	**2** snow	**3** cow
Diphthong Long **o**	Diphthong Long **o**	Diphthong Long **o**
4 bowl	**5** clown	**6** towel
Diphthong Long **o**	Diphthong Long **o**	Diphthong Long **o**
7 plow	**8** crown	**9** throw
Diphthong Long **o**	Diphthong Long **o**	Diphthong Long **o**
10 owl	**11** crow	**12** flowers
Diphthong Long **o**	Diphthong Long **o**	Diphthong Long **o**

LESSON 69: Recognizing Diphthong **ow**

141

The diphthong **ou** in **cloud** stands for the same vowel sound as the diphthong **ow** in **brown**. Circle the word that names each picture.

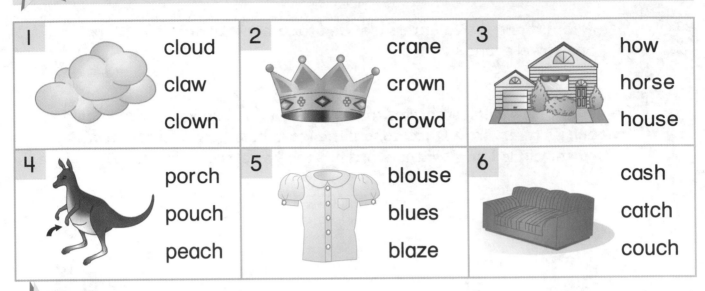

1		2		3	
	cloud		crane		how
	claw		crown		horse
	clown		crowd		house
4		5		6	
	porch		blouse		cash
	pouch		blues		catch
	peach		blaze		couch

Use a word from the box to complete each sentence.

brown	clouds	down	mountains	owl	sound

7. Let's go hiking in the _____.

8. Look up to see the _____ in the sky.

9. Look _____ to see the valleys below.

10. Sh! Don't make a _____.

11. Maybe we'll hear a _____ bear growling.

12. Maybe we'll hear a gray _____ hooting.

LESSON 69: Recognizing and Writing Diphthongs **ow** and **ou**

The diphthongs **oi** and **oy** stand for the vowel sound in **coins** and **boy**. The diphthong **ew** stands for the vowel sound in **screw**. Circle the word that names each picture.

1		2		3	
	cones coins cans		bow boy bee		crew stew screw

4		5		6	
	foil foul few		toes toys tows		boil bowl blew

The underlined word in each sentence does not make sense. Write a word from the box that would make sense.

enjoy	oil	news	soil	stew

7. You can plow the <u>spoil</u> and plant crops. _____

8. You can watch the <u>mew</u> to find out things. _____

9. You can put gas and <u>joy</u> in a car. _____

10. You can clap to show you <u>join</u> something. _____

11. You can put meat in a <u>flew</u>. _____

Write the name of each picture. Then find and circle the words in the puzzle. Look across and down.

1	 _____ ------ _____	2	 _____ ------ _____
3	 _____ ------ _____	4	 _____ ------ _____
5	 _____ ------ _____	6	 _____ ------ _____
7	 _____ ------ _____	8	 _____ ------ _____

```
b  r  o  w  n  d
o  a  t  o  y  s
y  f  o  i  l  c
c  l  o  u  d  r
c  o  w  b  c  e
h  o  u  s  e  w
```

Spell and Write

Say and spell each word in the box. Then write each word under the vowels in its name.

thread
spools
about
how
toys
news
saw
look
drew
because
join
brown

1
ea
_____
- - - - - - - - - - -
_____

2
oo
_____
- - - - - - - - - - -
_____

3
au
_____
- - - - - - - - - - -

aw
_____
- - - - - - - - - - -
_____

4
ow
_____
- - - - - - - - - - -
_____

ou
_____
- - - - - - - - - - -
_____

5
oi
_____
- - - - - - - - - - -

oy
_____
- - - - - - - - - - -

6
ew
_____
- - - - - - - - - - -
_____

 **Spell and Write** Think of something you can make from spools. Write a paragraph to describe it. Use one or more of your spelling words.

thread	spools	about	how	toys	news
saw	look	drew	because	join	brown

I can make

LESSON 71: Connecting Spelling and Writing

Look and Learn

Let's read and talk about colorful flowers.

bluebells

strawflowers

striped maple

Flowers can be many colors. Bluebells are blue, and so is ground ivy. Daisies and snowdrops are white. Some trees have green flowers and leaves. Strawflowers may be red, pink, yellow, violet, or white.

If you enjoy flowers, see if you can plant a garden. Watch it bloom into a rainbow. Watch for birds and butterflies that stop by.

If you had a garden, what would you plant in it? Why?

daisy

snowdrops

LESSON 72: Vowel Pairs, Vowel Digraphs, and Diphthongs in Context

147

Check-Up Circle the words in each list that have the same vowel sound as the picture name.

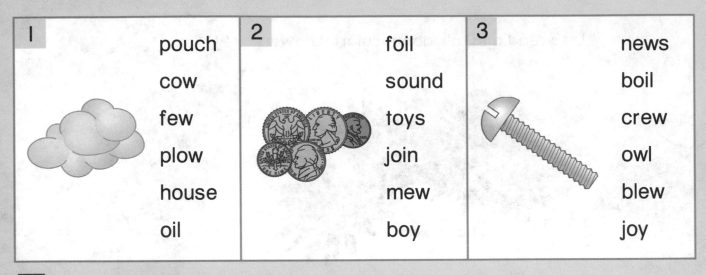

1	2	3
pouch	foil	news
cow	sound	boil
few	toys	crew
plow	join	owl
house	mew	blew
oil	boy	joy

Fill in the circle next to the word that completes the sentence. Write the word in the sentence.

4. Roy _____ painting pictures.

     ○ enjoys
     ○ boils

5. Joy likes looking at _____ .

     ○ sounds
     ○ clouds

6. Lew collects shiny new _____ .

     ○ coins
     ○ soil

7. Floyd collects _____ cars.

     ○ toy
     ○ joy

8. Joy stays up to watch the _____ .

     ○ news
     ○ mews

9. Sue enjoys milking the _____ .

     ○ couch
     ○ cow

10. Latoya helps make beef _____ .

     ○ stew
     ○ flew

NUMBERS, NUMBERS

Numbers in the grocery store
    About the things we eat,
Numbers on the doorways,
    And in the city street.

Numbers on the calendar,
    On signs that flash or glow,
Numbers on the telephone,
    Or tickets for the show.

Numbers on the buses,
    On money that I spend,
Numbers on the stamps I put
    On letters that I send.

Numbers on the highways, yes
    And numbers in a book!
It seems I'm seeing numbers
    Almost everywhere I look!

Lee Blair

Critical Thinking

Why are numbers important in your life?
What kinds of problems would people have
if there were no numbers?

Dear Family,

As your child progresses through this unit about numbers, he or she will learn about the following kinds of words and word endings.

---

contraction: two words written as one with one or more letters left out (**isn't = is not; I'll = I will**)

plural: word that means more than one (**book̲s̲, peach̲e̲s̲**)

word endings s, ed, ing: endings that can be added to a word to make new words (**need̲s̲, help̲e̲d̲, skipp̲e̲d̲, jump̲i̲n̲g̲, bak̲i̲n̲g̲**)

● Read the poem "Numbers, Numbers" on the reverse side.

● Look for plurals (**number̲s̲, thing̲s̲, doorway̲s̲, sign̲s̲, ticket̲s̲, buse̲s̲, stamp̲s̲, letter̲s̲, highway̲s̲**), contractions (**I'm**), and words that end in **ing** (**see̲i̲n̲g̲**).

● Talk about places where you see numbers.

Apreciada Familia:

En esta unidad, sobre los números, su niño aprenderá los siguientes tipos de palabras y terminaciones.

---

contracción: una palabra formada por la abreviación de dos palabras (**isn't = is not; I'll = I will**).

plural: palabras que indican más de uno (**book̲s̲, peach̲e̲s̲**).

palabras que terminan en s, ed, ing: letras que se añaden al final de una palabra (**need̲s̲, help̲e̲d̲, skipp̲e̲d̲, jump̲i̲n̲g̲, bak̲i̲n̲g̲**).

● Lea la poesía, "Numbers, Numbers" en la página 149.

● Busquen los plurales (**number̲s̲, thing̲s̲, doorway̲s̲, sign̲s̲, ticket̲s̲, buse̲s̲, stamp̲s̲, letter̲s̲, highway̲s̲**); una contracción (**I'm**); y la palabra que termina en **ing** (**see̲i̲n̲g̲**).

● Hablen de los lugares donde ven números.

PROJECT

Make a word bank by putting a slit in the top of a shoebox. Whenever your child learns a new contraction, plural word, or word that ends in **s**, **ed**, or **ing**, have him or her write the word on a card and "deposit" it in the bank. Your child can "withdraw" words and use them in sentences.

PROYECTO

Hagan un banco de palabras haciendo una abertura en la parte de arriba de una caja de zapatos. Cada vez que el niño aprenda una contracción, un plural, o una palabra que termine in **s**, **ed**, o **ing**, pídale escribir la palabra en una tarjeta y "depositarla" en el banco. El niño puede "retirar" palabras para escribir oraciones.

Helpful Hint

A **contraction** is a short way of writing two words as one. In a contraction, one or more letters are left out. An **apostrophe** (') shows where the letters were.

Didn't is the contraction for **did not**. **Won't** is the contraction for **will not**. Draw a line from each contraction to the pair of words that means the same.

1	didn't ●	● will not	5	isn't ●	● have not
2	won't ●	● could not	6	weren't ●	● does not
3	hasn't ●	● did not	7	haven't ●	● were not
4	couldn't ●	● has not	8	doesn't ●	● is not

Write the contraction for each pair of words.

aren't   don't   wasn't

can't   shouldn't   wouldn't

9 should not	10 was not	11 are not
12 can not	13 would not	14 do not

Taking Off

What would happen if there weren't any numbers? Write about it. Complete this sentence: "If there **weren't** any numbers, I **couldn't** . . . . ."

She'll is the contraction for **she will**. Draw a line from each contraction to the pair of words that means the same.

1	she'll ●	● we will	4	they'll ●	● I will
2	you'll ●	● she will	5	he'll ●	● he will
3	we'll ●	● you will	6	I'll ●	● they will

Write the contraction for the underlined words in each sentence. Then use the bus schedule to write two sentences of your own. Include a contraction in each sentence.

Place	Bus Number	Place	Bus Number
Zoo	57	Pine Lake	15
Downtown	25	Museum	32
Library	12	Skate Way	6
Central Park	30	South Mall	27

7. <u>I will</u> take Bus 12 to the library. _____

8. <u>She will</u> go downtown on Bus 25. _____

9. <u>He will</u> take Bus 15 to the lake. _____

10. Hurry or <u>you will</u> miss the bus! _____

11. _____

12. _____

LESSON 74: Recognizing and Writing Contractions with **will**

I'm is the contraction for **I am**. **He's** is the contraction for **he is**. **We're** is the contraction for **we are**. Write the contraction for each pair of words.

I'm	he's	you're	what's		it's
she's	we're	that's	they're		

1 I am _____	**2** he is _____	**3** we are _____
4 that is _____	**5** she is _____	**6** they are _____
7 it is _____	**8** what is _____	**9** you are _____

Write the words for the underlined contraction in each sentence.

10. I'm going to run in a race. _____

11. It's a two-mile run. _____

12. I hope you're planning to come. _____

She's is the contraction for **she is**. **She's** is also the contraction for **she has**. **You've** is the contraction for **you have**. **Let's** is the contraction for **let us**. Write the contraction for each pair of words.

I've	she's	let's	we've
he's	they've	you've	it's

1 she has	2 you have	3 let us

4 we have	5 he has	6 I have

7 they have	8 it has

Write the words for the underlined contraction in each sentence.

9. I've a new game we can play. _____

10. Watch Juan. He's played this game before. _____

11. Anita plays well. She's scored thirty points. _____

12. It's been fun playing this game with you. _____

LESSON 75: Recognizing and Writing Contractions with **have, has, us**

Spell and Write

Say and spell each word in the box. Then write each word under the correct heading.

didn't
you'll
I've
we've
that's
can't
let's
it's
I'll
what's
shouldn't
they've

1 Contractions with **not**

2 Contractions with **is**

3 Contractions with **have**

4 Contractions with **will**

5 Contraction with **us**

7:30 A.M.

Imagine that your classroom clock could talk. Write what it would say. Use one or more of your spelling words.

| didn't | you'll | I've | we've | that's | can't |
| let's | it's | I'll | what's | shouldn't | they've |

7:30 A.M.

Use the number code to write contractions. Write the letter for each number. Put an apostrophe in the blank space. Then write the words for each contraction.

1 = **a**	2 = **d**	3 = **e**	4 = **h**	5 = **i**
6 = **l**	7 = **n**	8 = **o**	9 = **r**	10 = **s**
11 = **t**	12 = **u**	13 = **v**	14 = **w**	15 = **y**

1 i s n ' t
   5 10 7   11

is   not

2 ___ ___ ___ ___
   14 3   13 3

3 ___ ___ ___ ___ ___
   15 8 12   9 3

4 ___ ___ ___ ___ ___
   10 4 3   6 6

5 ___ ___ ___ ___ ___
   2   5 2 7   11

6 ___ ___ ___ ___ ___ ___
   11 4 3 15   9 3

7 ___ ___ ___ ___ ___
   1   9 3 7   11

8 ___ ___ ___ ___ ___
   6   3 11   10

 **Check-Up** Draw a line from each contraction to the pair of words that means the same.

1	he'll ●	● she will	9	wasn't ●	● will not
2	she'll ●	● he has	10	you're ●	● was not
3	he's ●	● she has	11	won't ●	● you have
4	she's ●	● he will	12	you've ●	● you are
5	can't ●	● we are	13	I'm ●	● it has
6	couldn't ●	● can not	14	I've ●	● I will
7	we've ●	● could not	15	it's ●	● I am
8	we're ●	● we have	16	I'll ●	● I have

Underline the contraction in each sentence. Then write the words for the contraction.

17. What's your new room number? _____

18. I don't know mine yet. _____

19. Tony can't find his room. _____

20. I'll help him look for it. _____

21. I think it's down the hall. _____

Plural means "more than one." Add **s** to most words to make plurals. Add **es** to words that end in **s, ss, ch, sh, x,** or **z**.

Goats is the plural of **goat**. **Peaches** is the plural of **peach**. Each picture shows more than one. Add **s** or **es** to the word to write the picture name.

1	goat	2	peach
3	dish	4	shell
5	fox	6	cone
7	fork	8	dress
9	dime	10	bus

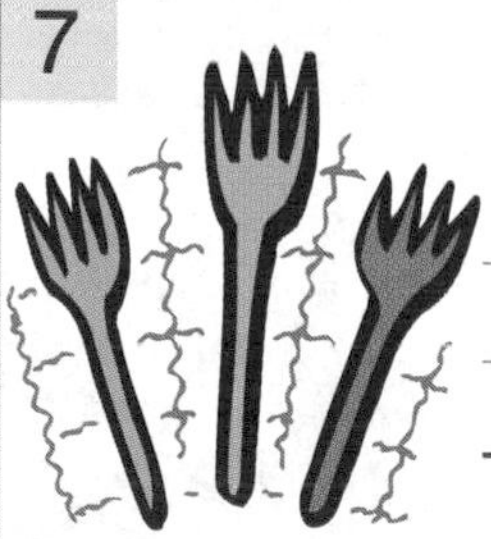

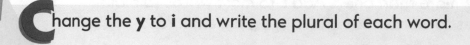

When a word ends in **y** after a consonant, change the **y** to **i** before adding **es**.

penny + es = pennies   baby + es= babies

Change the **y** to **i** and write the plural of each word.

1 penny	2 baby	3 party
4 story	5 puppy	6 fly

Add **es** to each word at the left and write the new word in the sentence.

puppy **7.** My dog Fleas had five _____.

baby **8.** Now they're as helpless as newborn _____.

pony **9.** Soon they'll be the size of small _____.

buddy **10.** The puppies and I are best _____.

penny **11.** Their fur is the color of shiny _____ !

Write the plural of each picture name in the puzzle. Remember to add **s** or **es** and to make spelling changes. Then read the shaded letters down to find the answer to the question.

1 ___ ___ ___ ___ ___ ___ ___

2 ___ ___ ___ ___ ___ ___

3 ___ ___ ___ ___ ___ ___

4 ___ ___ ___ ___ ___

5 ___ ___ ___ ___ ___

6 ___ ___ ___ ___ ___ ___

7 ___ ___ ___ ___ ___

8 ___ ___ ___ ___

9 ___ ___ ___ ___

10 ___ ___ ___ ___ ___

What number should you call in an emergency?

___ ___ ___

___ ___ ___

___ ___ ___

Check-Up Add **s** or **es** to write the plural of each word. Remember to make spelling changes.

1 pony	2 trunk	3 dress
_____	_____	_____
_____	_____	_____

4 box	5 sack	6 fly
_____	_____	_____
_____	_____	_____

7 bunny	8 peach	9 straw
_____	_____	_____
_____	_____	_____

Add **s** or **es** so that the word in **bold** print makes sense in each sentence.

10. There are 10 **penny** in a dime.   _____

11. **Mayfly** live only about 2 hours.   _____

12. **Fox** live only 7 years.   _____

13. Newborn **baby** have 300 bones.   _____

14. There are more than 12,000 kinds of **ant**.   _____

Helpful Hint

A **base** word is a word to which endings like **s** and **es** may be added to make new words.

help + s = helps   fix + es = fixes

Add **s** or **es** to each base word. Write the new word.

1 help	2 fix
3 brush	4 buzz
5 find	6 mix

Underline the word ending in **s** or **es** in each sentence. Write the base word.

7. Nikki hits the ball with a crack. _____

8. She quickly drops the bat. _____

9. Nikki rushes past Jenny. _____

10. She reaches first base safely. _____

When a base word ends in **y** after a consonant, change the **y** to **i** before adding **es**.

hurry + es = hurries   try + es = tries

1 hurry _____	**2** try _____
3 fry _____	**4** carry _____
5 copy _____	**6** study _____

Use a word from above to complete each sentence. Then read the story.

Dan is always in a hurry. He _____

home from school. He _____ a bag of

books. He _____ for an hour. He neatly

_____ over his book report. He always

_____ to finish quickly. Then he hurries out to play.

The endings **ing** and **ed** can be added to a base word.
help + ing = helping   help + ed = helped

Add **ing** to each base word. Write the new word.

1	help _____	2	fix _____
3	jump _____	4	grow _____
5	find _____	6	pass _____

Underline the word ending in **ing** in each sentence.
Write the base word.

7. June is helping Azeem do math.   _____

8. They are adding numbers.   _____

9. June and Azeem are trying to solve a problem.   _____

10. They like working together.   _____

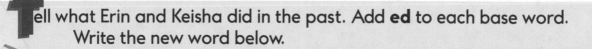

Tell what Erin and Keisha did in the past. Add **ed** to each base word. Write the new word below.

Things Erin Did at the Lake	Things Keisha Did in the Kitchen

Things Erin Did at the Lake

sail   splash   surf   float

1 _____

2 _____

3 _____

4 _____

Things Keisha Did in the Kitchen

wash   broil   mix   cook

5 _____

6 _____

7 _____

8 _____

Add **ed** to each base word and write the new word in the sentence.

want   **9.** Jon _____ to speak to his friend Abdul.

look   **10.** He _____ for Abdul's number.

push   **11.** He _____ the buttons on the phone.

reach   **12.** Jon _____ Abdul's home.

ask   **13.** He _____ to speak to Abdul.

Helpful Hint

When a base word ends in **e,** drop the final **e** before adding **ing** or **ed**.
smile + ing = smiling   smile + ed = smiled

Drop the final **e** and add **ing** to each base word.
Write the new word.

1	smile	**2**	serve	**3**	dance
4	bake	**5**	hide	**6**	sneeze

Add **ing** to a word from the box to complete each sentence.

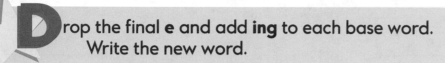

drive	pave	take	wave

7. Mr. Lange is _____ home on Route 80.

8. He's _____ a shortcut.

9. Uh-oh! There's someone _____ a flag.

10. Workers are _____ the road.

LESSON 82: Dropping Final **e** Before Adding Inflectional Ending **ing**

167

Tell what Brad and Alicia did in the past. Drop the final **e** and add **ed** to each base word. Write the new word below.

Things Brad Did at Home

	bake rake bike slice
1	
2	
3	
4	

Things Alicia Did at School

	trace tape erase race
5	
6	
7	
8	

Read the first sentence in each pair. Complete the second sentence so that it tells about the past. Drop the final **e** and add **ed** to the underlined word.

9. I <u>skate</u> at the ice rink every day.

_____

Yesterday I _____ until 5:00 P.M.

10. I always <u>race</u> my friends.

_____

Last Tuesday I _____ my two sisters.

11. I also <u>dance</u> on the ice.

_____

Last week I _____ for 15 minutes.

Talking Off

Tell how you usually spend time with your friends.
Tell what you did last week.

If a short vowel word ends in a single consonant, usually double the final consonant before adding **ing** or **ed**.

jog + ing = jogging   **jog + ed = jogged**

Double the final consonant and add **ing** to each base word. Write the new word.

1	2	3
jog	skip	wag

4	5	6
knit	cut	grab

Underline the word ending in **ing** in each sentence. Write the base word.

7. Jim is swimming laps in the pool. _____

8. He swims back and forth without stopping. _____

9. Jim is getting lots of exercise. _____

10. He is planning to swim six laps tomorrow. _____

Tell about the past. Add **ed** to a word from the box to complete each sentence. Then read the story.

| clap | hum | tap | plan | pat |

Last summer our town had a frog-jumping contest.

I p_____ to win with my frog Tiny. I knew just

what to do. At the start, I t_____ Tiny on the

head for good luck. I also h_____ a good-luck

song. Then I p_____ Tiny on the back to get

him started.

On his first jump, Tiny leaped eleven feet! I

c_____ and jumped up and down.

What happened on Tiny's second and third jumps? Finish the story.

_____

_____

_____

_____

_____

LESSON 83: Doubling Final Consonant Before Adding Inflectional Ending **ed**

Helpful Hint

Some words end in l**e**.

Apple ends in **le**. Find the name of each picture. Write the word.

apple	needle	rattle	ankle	eagle	candle
table	bottle	pickle	circle	turtle	purple

1.

2.

3.

4.

5.

6.

7.

8.

9.

10.

11.

12.

LESSON 84: Recognizing and Writing Words Ending in **le**

171

Write each word under the correct heading.

bugle   crackle   huddle   juggle
    rattle   tumble   sizzle   wiggle

1 Things to Do	2 Things to Hear

Underline the words that end in **le**. Then circle **Yes** or **No** to answer each question.

3. Can you draw a circle inside a triangle?   Yes   No

4. Can you buckle a bubble?   Yes   No

5. Can an eagle juggle?   Yes   No

6. Can people do puzzles?   Yes   No

7. Does a poodle have a rattle?   Yes   No

8. Can an ankle giggle?   Yes   No

9. Can a turtle swim in a puddle?   Yes   No

10. Can bells jingle and jangle?   Yes   No

LESSON 84: Recognizing and Writing Words Ending in **le**

When a base word ends in **y** after a consonant, change the **y** to **i** before adding **ed**.

hurry + ed = hurried   **carry + ed = carried**

Tell about the past. Change **y** to **i** and add **ed** to each base word. Write the new word.

1	hurry	2	carry	3	try
4	dry	5	copy	6	cry

Combine words from boxes A, B, and C to write three sentences about the past.

A		B		C	
Last week		Marina		fried fish.	
Yesterday		Dennis		dried dishes.	
On Monday		Fran		studied spelling.	

Complete each column by adding the ending at the top
to the base word.

	s or es	ing	ed
1 paint			
2 rush			
3 chase			
4 try			

Write the base word.

5 sleeps	6 winning	7 flipped
8 making	9 pitches	10 saved
11 quitting	12 dries	13 studied

Spell and Write

Say and spell each word in the box. Then write each word under the correct heading.

brushes

carried

hurried

jogging

jumping

raked

running

smiling

stopped

tries

washed

wiped

1 No Base Changes

_____
_____
_____
_____
_____

2 Change y to i

_____
_____
_____
_____
_____

3 Drop Final e

_____
_____
_____
_____
_____

4 Double Final Consonant

_____
_____
_____
_____
_____

Spell and Write Read the playground rhyme. Then add one or two verses. Use one or more of your spelling words.

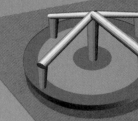

| brushes | carried | hurried | jogging | jumping | raked |
| running | smiling | stopped | tries | washed | wiped |

I went outside to count the stars.
I made a mistake and counted cars.
I went inside to bake a pie.
I made a mistake and baked a fly.

Look and Learn

Let's read and talk about clocks.

What time is it? Let's look at a clock to find out. Analog clocks have faces with numbers 1 to 12 and hands that point to the minutes and the hour. Digital clocks don't have hands. The hour and the minutes are separated by a : . The number before the : tells the hour. The number after the : tells the minutes past the hour.

What would happen if people didn't have clocks or watches?

177

 **Add the ending at the top to each base word in the column.**

s or es	ing	ed
1. clean _____	4. bake _____	7. stop _____
2. mix _____	5. know _____	8. jump _____
3. cry _____	6. drip _____	9. wipe _____

Underline the word ending in **ing** or **ed** in each sentence. Then write the base word.

10. Mai Lin was enjoying a dream. _____

11. At 7:00 A.M., her alarm clock buzzed. _____

12. She reached for the clock on the table. _____

13. With her eyes closed, she couldn't find it. _____

14. Where was the clock hiding? _____

15. Mai Lin tried to go back to sleep. _____

Swinging

Slowly, slowly, swinging low,
Let me see how far I go!
Slowly, slowly, keeping low,
I see where the wild flowers grow!

(Getting quicker):
Quicker, quicker,
Swinging higher,
I can see
A shining spire!
Quicker, quicker,
Swinging higher,
I can see
The sunset's fire!

Faster, faster,
Through the air,
I see almost
Everywhere.
Woods and hills,
And sheep that stare—
And things I never
Knew were there!

(Getting slower):
Slower, slower, now I go,
Swinging, dreaming, getting low;
Slowly, slowly, down I go—
Till I touch the grass below.

Irene Thompson

Critical Thinking

What do you think is the best part about going high on a swing?
If you could put a swing anywhere, where would you put it? Why?

8

LESSON 88: Introduction to Suffixes, Prefixes, Synonyms, Antonyms, and Homonyms

179

Dear Family,

As your child progresses through this unit about outdoor fun, she or he will learn about the following kinds of word parts and words.

suffix: word part added to the end of a word to change its meaning or make a new word (care**ful**)

prefix: word part added to the beginning of a word to change its meaning or make a new word (**re**load)

synonyms: words that have the same meaning (**fast/quick**)

antonyms: words that have the opposite meaning (**up/down**)

homonyms: words that sound the same but have different spellings and meanings (**blue/blew**)

- Read the poem "Swinging" on the reverse side.
- Look for words with the suffixes **ly** and **er** (slow**ly**, quick**er**, high**er**, fast**er**, slow**er**). Also look for synonyms (**quicker/faster**) and antonyms (**quicker/slower, faster/slower**).
- Talk about ways you and your family have outdoor fun.

PROJECT

Help your child draw a kite and cut it out. Attach a tail. Encourage your child to write new words on small pieces of paper and tape them to the tail.

Apreciada Familia:

En esta unidad, sobre el recreo, su niño aprenderá otros tipos de palabras y partes de palabras.

sufijos: letras que se añaden al final de una palabra y que cambian su significado o hace una nueva (care**ful**).

prefijos: letras que se añaden al principio de una palabra y que cambian su significado o hacen una nueva (**re**load).

sinónimos: palabras que tienen el mismo significado (**fast/quick**).

antónimos: palabras que significan lo opuesto (**up/down**).

homónimos: palabras que tienen el mismo sonido pero diferente significado y se escriben diferentes (**blue/blew**).

- Lea,"Swinging" en la página 179.
- Busquen palabras que tengan los sufijos **ly, er** (slow**ly**, quick**er**, high**er**, fast**er**, slow**er**). Busquen los sinónimos (**quicker/faster**) y los antónimos (**quicker/slower, faster/slower**).
- Hablen de lo que hace su familia para divertiese fuera de la casa.

PROYECTO

Ayude a su niño a dibujar y recortar una cometa. Atele una cola. Anime al niño a escribir palabras en pedacitos de papel y pegarlas en la cola de la cometa.

up

down

untie

useful

A **suffix** is a word part added to the **end** of a base word to change its meaning or make a new word.

fear + ful = fearful   fear + less = fearless
soft + ness = softness   soft + ly = softly

The suffix **ful** means "full of." **Fearful** means "full of fear." Add the suffix **ful** to each base word. Write the new word below.

Words that Describe People or Things

help   grace   play   use

1 _____

2 _____

3 _____

4 _____

Words that Describe Feelings

cheer   fear   hope   thank

5 _____

6 _____

7 _____

8 _____

Write about the puppy. Use a word that ends in the suffix **ful**.

_____

_____

_____

cloudless	darkness	fearless	loudness	softness	useless

1 without fear	2 being soft	3 being loud
_____	_____	_____
_____	_____	_____

4 without use	5 without clouds	6 being dark
_____	_____	_____
_____	_____	_____

Use a word from above to complete each sentence.

7. Cleo is a brave and _____ hunter.

8. Don't be fooled by the _____ of her fur.

9. Don't be fooled by the _____ of her purr.

10. It's _____ to try to keep her indoors.

11. She goes out and hunts on sunny, _____ days.

12. She goes out and hunts in the _____ of the night.

The suffix **ly** means "in a certain way." **Softly** means "in a soft way." Add the suffix **ly** to a base word from the box and write a new word to answer the question.

bright	soft	loud	glad

1. How does snow fall? _____

2. How does the sun shine? _____

3. How does thunder boom? _____

4. How do you greet a friend? _____

brave	sweet	slow	quick

5. How does a snail crawl? _____

6. How does a hero act? _____

7. How does a deer run? _____

8. How does a bird sing? _____

Write a question of your own that can be answered with a word that ends in **ly**. Exchange questions with a classmate.

Find and write the word that goes with each definition.

bravely	cheerful	fearless	hopeful	loudness
slowly	kindness	sadly	useless	

1 without fear

_____

_____

2 being loud

_____

_____

3 in a slow way

_____

_____

4 full of cheer

_____

_____

5 in a sad way

_____

_____

6 without use

_____

_____

7 being kind

_____

_____

8 full of hope

_____

_____

9 in a brave way

_____

_____

Add the suffix **ful, less, ness,** or **ly** so the word in **bold** print makes sense in each sentence. Write the new word.

_____

10. Julie waited for a **cloud** night.   _____

11. She **quick** set up her telescope.   _____

12. She saw the stars shining **bright**.   _____

13. They twinkled in the **dark**.   _____

184   LESSON 90: Reviewing Suffixes **ful, less, ness, ly**

Helpful Hint

The suffix **er** is added to a base word to compare two things.
The suffix **est** is added to compare more than two things.

small   small**er**   small**est**

Compare the things. Add **er** or **est** to the base word and write the new word.

1	2	3

small

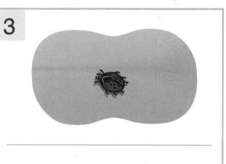

Add **er** and **est** to each base word. Write the new word.

	er	est
4. fast		
5. cold		
6. soft		
7. kind		

Taking Off

Write three sentences to describe a race between a turtle, a snail, and an inchworm. Use the words **slow, slower,** and **slowest**.

LESSON 91: Writing Suffixes **er** and **est**

© William H. Sadlier, Inc. All rights reserved.

Sometimes you need to make spelling changes before adding **er** or **est**.
wet + er = wetter   wet + est = wettest
sunny + er = sunnier   sunny + est = sunniest

Double the final consonant and add **er** and **est** to each word.
Write the new words.

er	est

1. wet

2. thin

3. big

4. hot

Change the **y** to **i** and add **er** and **est** to each word.
Write the new words.

er	est

5. sunny

6. bumpy

7. happy

8. lucky

Draw a picture to show the meaning of **wet, wetter, wettest**.
Write three sentences to go with it.

Read the first sentence in each pair. Complete the second sentence by adding **er** or **est** to the word in **bold** print. Remember to make spelling changes if you need to.

1 Rabbits, zebras, and lions all run **fast**.

_____

The lion is the _____ of the three animals.

2 Milly swings up **high** into the sky.

_____

Mat swings up _____ .

3 Jack is **tall**.

_____

Jill is even _____ .

4 90°F is **hot**.

_____

95°F is _____ .

5 All the pencils are **thick**.

_____

The first pencil is the _____ .

6 Sometimes Zach is a **messy** eater.

_____

His baby sister is _____ .

Use the suffix **ful, less, ness,** or **ly** to write a word for each definition.

1 full of fear	2 in a slow way	3 without use
4 being dark	5 without a cloud	6 full of cheer
7 in a brave way	8 without fear	9 being loud
10 full of hope	11 in a quick way	12 being soft

nderline the word in parentheses that makes sense in each sentence.

13. It was the (**hottest, hotter**) day of the year.

14. I (**gladly, sadly**) agreed to go for a ride with Uncle Al.

15. We went up (**highest, high**) in the sky in a hot air balloon.

16. We flew over the (**taller, tallest**) of all the trees.

17. We flew (**faster, fast**) than the wind.

18. My brother thinks I'm a (**cloudless, fearless**) person.

19. I think I'm the (**luckiest, luckier**) person in the world.

20. I will always remember my uncle's (**kindness, softness**).

A **prefix** is a word part added to the **beginning** of a base word to change its meaning or make a new word.

re + tie = retie   **un + happy = unhappy**   **dis + honest = dishonest**

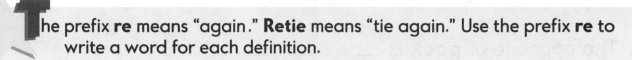

The prefix **re** means "again." **Retie** means "tie again." Use the prefix **re** to write a word for each definition.

1 tie again	2 tell again	3 join again
4 place again	5 fill again	6 pack again
7 load again	8 use again	9 check again

Add the prefix **re** to each base word and write the new word in the sentence.

pack   **10.** Josh had to _____ his backpack.

fill   **11.** Deb had to _____ the canteens.

tie   **12.** We'll leave as soon as I _____ my shoe.

The prefix **un** means "not" or "to do the opposite of." **Unhappy** means "not happy." **Unpack** is the opposite of **pack**. Add the prefix **un** to the word in **bold** print to complete each sentence.

1. Someone who is not **happy** is _____.

2. The opposite of **pack** is _____.

3. If something is not **safe**, it's _____.

4. The opposite of **button** is _____.

5. If you are not **able** to swim, you are _____ to swim.

6. The opposite of **roll** is _____.

Add the prefix **un** to each base word and write the new word in the sentence.

safe   7. Without a helmet, skating is _____.

able   8. I've looked, but I'm _____ to find my helmet.

pack   9. I guess I'll _____ my skating gear.

roll   10. I'll _____ my sleeping bag and camp out instead.

The prefix **dis** means "not" or "do the opposite of." **Dishonest** means "not honest." **Disagree** is the opposite of **agree**. Use the prefix **dis** to write a word for each definition.

1 not honest	2 the opposite of **agree**	3 the opposite of **obey**
4 the opposite of **like**	5 not pleased	6 the opposite of **appear**

Add the prefix **dis** so that the word in **bold** print makes sense in each sentence. Write the new word.

7. Jen and I are friends even when we **agree**. _____

8. I get upset when my dog **obeys** me. _____

9. It is **honest** to tell a lie. _____

10. Snow **appears** when it gets hot. _____

Write one thing you **like** and one thing you **dislike** about the outdoors.

Write the base word for each word.

1 replay	2 untie	3 displease
_____	_____	_____
4 unsafe	5 distrust	6 repaint
_____	_____	_____
7 disagree	8 rejoin	9 unafraid
_____	_____	_____

Fill in the circle next to the prefix that completes the word and makes sense in the sentence.

10. Let's take pictures before the sun ___appears.   ○ dis ○ un

11. Here's a good spot to ___pack our bags.   ○ un ○ dis

12. We'll ___load the camera so we don't run out of film. ○ dis ○ re

13. Hold still or the pictures will be ___clear.   ○ re ○ un

14. That's a good shot of a boy ___locking his bike.   ○ un ○ dis

15. It's time to ___pack our bags and head home.   ○ dis ○ re

Write a word with the prefix **re, un,** or **dis** for each clue. Then read the shaded letters down to find the answer to the question.

1 join again ___ ___ ___ ___ ___ ___

2 opposite of **tie** ___ ___ ___ ___ ___

3 opposite of **trust** ___ ___ ___ ___ ___ ___ ___

4 draw again ___ ___ ___ ___ ___ ___

5 opposite of **load** ___ ___ ___ ___ ___

6 opposite of **obey** ___ ___ ___ ___ ___ ___ ___

7 not true ___ ___ ___ ___ ___ ___

8 fill again ___ ___ ___ ___ ___ ___

9 use again ___ ___ ___ ___ ___

10 not able ___ ___ ___ ___ ___ ___

What can you do in the summer sun?

_____ _____

Have a lot of _____ _____ !

Check-Up Write the base word for each word.

1 retell	2 unpack	3 disobey

4 untie	5 disagree	6 recheck

7 dishonest	8 refill	9 unbutton

nderline the word in parentheses that makes sense in each sentence.

10. Mom says that my treehouse is (**unable, unsafe**).

11. That (**disagrees, displeases**) Mom.

12. It makes me (**unhappy, unroll**), too.

13. We have to (**reuse, replace**) wood that has rotted.

14. We have to (**repaint, replay**) the whole thing.

15. We have to (**reload, retie**) the rope ladder.

16. I (**dislike, disappear**) scratchy sandpaper.

17. I'm (**untied, unable**) to reach the roof.

18. It's (**unclear, unafraid**) how we'll ever finish.

19. I wish I could (**disappear, distrust**) now!

20. I'd better stop complaining and (**refill, rejoin**) Mom at work.

Synonyms are words that have the same or nearly the same meaning.

Fast and **quick** are synonyms. Find and write a synonym for each word.

jog	begin	fast	home	large	bag

1	quick	2	run	3	start

4	big	5	sack	6	house

Draw a line from each word in the first column to its synonym in the second column.

7	jump	●	● happy	13	cry	●	● weep
8	rush	●	● leap	14	sound	●	● high
9	glad	●	● hurry	15	tall	●	● noise
10	boat	●	● kind	16	wet	●	● yell
11	nice	●	● close	17	sick	●	● ill
12	near	●	● ship	18	shout	●	● damp

Circle the word in each list that means the same or nearly the same as the word in **bold** print.

1 home	2 below	3 leave	4 pail
door	over	stay	bucket
house	in	here	spoon
car	under	go	water
work	out	slow	sink

Write the word from the box that is a synonym for the word in **bold** print.

hike	likes	little	pal	tapped	trail

5. My **friend** Goldie likes to walk in the woods. _____

6. She **enjoys** collecting leaves. _____

7. One day Goldie went for a **walk**. _____

8. She decided to explore a new **path**. _____

9. She followed the path to a **small** house. _____

10. Goldie **knocked** on the door. _____

Was anyone home? Finish the story. In your sentences, you might use synonyms for the words **big** and **small**.

LESSON 96: Recognizing and Writing Synonyms

Antonyms are words that have the opposite or nearly the opposite meaning.

Hot and **cold** are antonyms. Find and write an antonym for each word.

big	smile	hot	open	under
stop	left	float	asleep	

1 cold	2 awake	3 right
_____	_____	_____

4 go	5 little	6 over
_____	_____	_____

7 frown	8 sink	9 close
_____	_____	_____

Circle the word in each list that means the opposite of the word in **bold** print.

10 **happy**	11 **clean**	12 **lost**	13 **front**
good	water	gone	back
glad	wash	found	door
sad	dirty	under	top

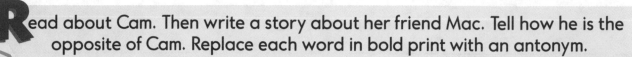

Cam is a **tall girl**. **She** sits in the **last** row of **her** class. **She** has **long** hair and freckles. **She always** wears glasses. When **she** writes, **she** uses **her right** hand.

Cam likes **winter** sports. **She** enjoys skating. Even on the **coldest** days, you'll find Cam outdoors.

Mac is a short boy.

Homonyms are words that sound the same but have different spellings and meanings.

Sail and **sale** are homonyms. Find and write a homonym for each word.

sun	for	sail	ate	to	not

1 sale _____	2 eight _____	3 knot _____
4 four _____	5 son _____	6 two _____

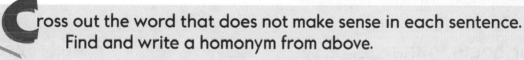

Cross out the word that does not make sense in each sentence. Find and write a homonym from above.

7. I eight breakfast early in the morning. _____

8. Then I decided to go four a walk. _____

9. The son was shining brightly. _____

10. It was a great day two be outdoors. _____

1 tale tall		**2** ride right		**3** reed road	
tail tell		write white		ride rode	
4 knot note		**5** dear deep		**6** weed weak	
night knight		deer deal		week wood	

Circle and write the word that completes each sentence.

7. Lashanda and I _____ little toy boats.   made   maid

8. Mine was red and hers was _____.   blew   blue

9. We put paper _____ on the top.   sales   sails

10. We put our boats in the _____.   creek   creak

11. We decided to race _____ boats.   hour   our

12. The wind _____ the sails.   blew   blue

13. Lashanda and _____ clapped.   eye   I

14. Lashanda _____ the race.   one   won

Write a word from the box for each clue in the puzzle.

cry	fast	first	hot	lost	plain
rode	sale	sea	stop	under	wet

ACROSS ➡

1. Opposite of **go**
4. Opposite of **slow**
5. Means **below**

DOWN ⬇

1. Sounds like **see**
2. Sounds like **plane**
3. Means **damp**

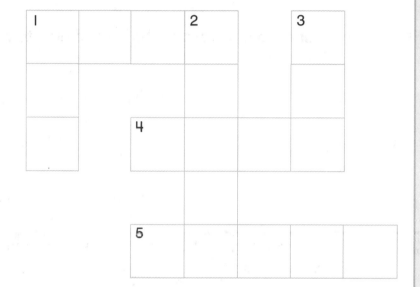

ACROSS ➡

6. Opposite of **last**
10. Opposite of **found**
11. Sounds like **road**

DOWN ⬇

7. Sounds like **sail**
8. Opposite of **cold**
9. Means **weep**

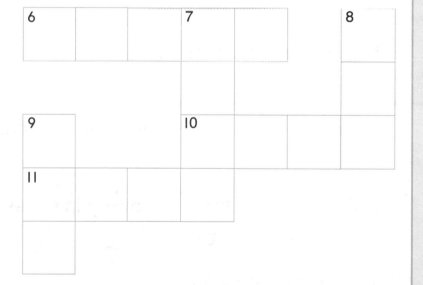

Write a sentence using two or more homonyms. For example, "We **rode** down the **road** and saw a **plane** land on the **plain**."

LESSON 99: Reviewing Synonyms, Antonyms, and Homonyms

Draw a line from a word in the first column to its synonym in the second column.

1	home ●	● nap	4	bag ●		● begin
2	sleep ●	● ill	5	friend ●		● pal
3	sick ●	● house	6	start ●		● sack

Draw a line from a word in the first column to its antonym in the second column.

7	little ●	● front	10	out ●		● open
8	long ●	● big	11	close ●		● in
9	back ●	● short	12	awake ●		● asleep

Cross out the word that does not make sense in each sentence. Find and write the correct word.

I	new	to	made	wood

13. Dad maid a swing for me.

_____

14. He used a piece of would for the seat.

_____

15. Dad and eye hung the swing in a tree.

_____

16. I like my knew swing.

_____

17. Watch me swing two and fro.

_____

_____

Spell and Write Say and spell each word in the box.
Then write six pairs of homonyms.

word box
new
blew
sale
too
for
to
knew
night
sail
knight
blue
four

1 _____

2 _____

3 _____

4 _____

5 _____

6 _____

LESSON 100: Connecting Spelling and Writing   **203**

Write a poem about summer. Use one or more of your spelling words.

new	blew	sale	too	for	to
knew	night	sail	knight	blue	four

LESSON 100: Connecting
Spelling and Writing

Look and Learn

Let's read and talk about
Grand Canyon National Park.

20¢

It's the biggest. It's the oldest. It's the most unusual. It's Grand Canyon National Park, and it's filled with things to do. You can take a tour bus. You can take a boat. If you're twelve years old, you can ride a mule. Anyone can choose a trail and go for a hike. But don't go too far. Remember that after you walk down, you have to climb back up!

Think about hiking down into the Grand Canyon. What would be fun? What would be difficult?

JUN 30 · ARIZONA · GRAND CANYON

LESSON 101: Suffixes, Prefixes, Synonyms, Antonyms, and Homonyms in Context

205

Circle the word in each list that means the **same** or **nearly the same** as the word in **bold** print.

1 **run**	2 **big**	3 **glad**	4 **shout**
walk	small	sleepy	yell
legs	large	happy	whisper
jog	thin	sad	talk

5 **begin**	6 **rush**	7 **noise**	8 **quick**
write	soon	hear	slow
start	go	quiet	fast
end	hurry	sound	still

Circle two words in each row that have **opposite** meanings.

9.	stop	look	car	go
10.	door	front	back	open
11.	smooth	clean	garden	dirty
12.	in	out	last	next
13.	left	new	quiet	right
14.	below	lost	found	weak

Circle two words in each box that **sound the same** but have different spellings and meanings.

15	mad	made	16	knot	not	17	reed	ride
	mud	maid		note	knit		road	rode

18	door	dear	19	blew	blend	20	tall	tail
	deer	do		blind	blue		tell	tale

206   LESSON 101: Assessing Synonyms, Antonyms, and Homonyms

STUDENT SKILLS
ASSESSMENT CHECKLIST

☑ Assessed ☒ Retaught ◼ Mastered

Unit 1

Initial, Medial, and Final Consonants
- ❑ Initial Consonants
- ❑ Final Consonants
- ❑ Medial Consonants

Unit 2

Short Vowels
- ❑ Short Vowel **a**
- ❑ Short Vowel **i**
- ❑ Short Vowel **o**
- ❑ Short Vowel **u**
- ❑ Short Vowel **e**

Unit 3

Long Vowels
- ❑ Long Vowel **a**
- ❑ Long Vowel **i**
- ❑ Long Vowel **o**
- ❑ Long Vowel **u**
- ❑ Long Vowel **e**

Unit 4

Variant Consonant Sounds and Consonant Blends
- ❑ Soft and Hard **c**
- ❑ Soft and Hard **g**
- ❑ Initial **l**-blends
- ❑ Initial **r**-blends
- ❑ Initial **s**-blends
- ❑ Final Consonant Blends

Unit 5

Compound Words, y as a Vowel, Consonant Digraphs, and r-controlled Vowels
- ❑ Compound Words
- ❑ Two-Syllable Words
- ❑ **y** as a Vowel
- ❑ Initial Consonant Digraphs **th, sh, wh, ch**
- ❑ Final Consonant Digraphs **ck, th, sh, ch**
- ❑ Consonant Digraph **kn**
- ❑ Consonant Digraph **wr**
- ❑ **ar**-words
- ❑ **or**-words
- ❑ **er**-words, **ir**-words, **ur**-words

Teacher Comments

Unit 6

Vowel Pairs, Vowel Digraphs, and Diphthongs
- ❑ Vowel Pairs **ai** and **ay**
- ❑ Vowel Pairs **ea** and **ee**
- ❑ Vowel Pairs **oa, ow, oe**
- ❑ Vowel Pairs **ui, ue, ie**
- ❑ Vowel Digraph **ea**
- ❑ Vowel Digraph **oo**
- ❑ Vowel Digraphs **au** and **aw**
- ❑ Diphthongs **ow** and **ou**
- ❑ Diphthongs **oi, oy, ew**

Unit 7

Contractions and Word Endings
- ❑ Contractions with **not**
- ❑ Contractions with **will**
- ❑ Contractions with **am, is, are**
- ❑ Contractions with **have, has, us**
- ❑ Plural Endings **s** and **es**
- ❑ Changing **y** to **i** Before Adding Plural Ending **es**
- ❑ Inflectional Endings **s** and **es**
- ❑ Changing **y** to **i** Before Adding Inflectional Ending **es**
- ❑ Inflectional Ending **ing**
- ❑ Inflectional Ending **ed**
- ❑ Dropping Final **e** Before Adding **ing**
- ❑ Dropping Final **e** Before Adding **ed**
- ❑ Doubling Final Consonant Before Adding **ing**
- ❑ Doubling Final Consonant Before Adding **ed**
- ❑ Words Ending in **le**
- ❑ Changing **y** to **i** Before Adding **ed**

Unit 8

Suffixes, Prefixes, Synonyms, Antonyms, and Homonyms
- ❑ Suffix **ful**
- ❑ Suffixes **less** and **ness**
- ❑ Suffix **ly**
- ❑ Suffixes **er** and **est**
- ❑ Spelling Changes Before Adding **er** and **est**
- ❑ Prefix **re**
- ❑ Prefix **un**
- ❑ Prefix **dis**
- ❑ Synonyms
- ❑ Antonyms
- ❑ Homonyms

Name _____

Friends of Mine

Jan is my pen pal. We write letters to each other.

Kareem is my buddy. We ride bikes together on Saturdays.

Think about your best friend and what you like to do together. Then draw a picture.

Fold

Fold

1

3

8

9

Directions: Help your child cut and fold the book. Read it together several times. Have your child identify beginning and ending consonants.

UNIT 1: Take-home Book

Name

Water's Song

Fold

3

Water lapping on the sand.

Seas carrying giant ships
Taking people on long trips.

8

Fold

Oceans sending pretty shells.

9

Directions: Help your child cut and fold the book. Read it together several times.
Have your child find the rhyming words. Ask what vowel sounds are in the words.

4

Raindrops falling on city blocks,

2

Rivers cutting through the land,

Fold

Waves crashing on ocean rocks.

Water pumped from farmers' wells.

Fold

4
5

7

Name _____

Tree Leaves and Seeds

1

Pine trees and blue spruce have needles for leaves. They keep their leaves all year.

3

Draw a picture of a leaf or a seed.
Write its name.

8

Some seeds are inside fruit.
Can you describe the seed of an apple, an orange, a lime, a date, or a peach?

6

Directions: Help your child cut and fold the book. Read it together several times.
Have your child find words with vowels that say their own names.

UNIT 3: Take-home Book

213

4

2

There are many different trees. Each kind of tree has a different leaf.

oak leaf

pine needles

maple leaf

Fold

Fold

Some trees, like oaks and maples, lose their leaves in the fall. New leaves grow back in the spring.

oak

maple

elm

Most trees grow from seeds.

Some seeds are nuts. Walnuts, pecans, almonds and Brazil nuts are all seeds.

almond

walnut

Brazil nut

pecan

7

5

Name _____

City Beat

Cars and trucks are slow or fast,
Blocks of people move right past.
Slow—fast—move right past.

Uptown, downtown, children say,
It's the place to live and play.
Uptown—downtown—live and play.

Lights are blinking, high and low,
Red means stop, green means go.
Red—green—stop and go.

DON'T WALK
WALK

Directions: Help your child cut and fold the book. Read it together several times.
Have your child find words with consonant blends like **tr** and **sp** and words
with soft and hard **c** and **g** like **cent**, **cat**, **gym**, and **goat**.

UNIT 4: Take-home Book

Giant buildings made of brick,
Elevators go up quick.
Up—down—make it quick!

Boys and girls from east and west
Think the city is the best.
East—west—city's best.

Under streets, down below,
Trains with folks go to and fro.
Trains—folks—to and fro.

Music, dancing, friends to meet,
Spinning feet step to the beat.
Sing—dance—to the beat.

Name _____

Magic Carpet Ride

Inside the trunk under some shirts was a purple carpet. The note on the carpet said, "I will take you anywhere you wish to go." 3

If you had a magic carpet, where would you go? Draw a picture and write about it.

8

Then the children visited China. They saw a furry panda eating bamboo. 6

Directions: Help your child cut and fold the book. Read it together several times. Have your child find words with consonant digraphs **th, sh, wh, ch, ck, wr**, and **kn**. Look for compound words and words with **ar, or, ir**, and **ur**.

UNIT 5: Take-home Book

2

One rainy afternoon, Theo and Barb went up to the attic to explore. They found a big, black trunk in the corner.

4

"Let's go to the Rocky Mountains," said Theo. With a swish, they began to fly over the treetops. They landed on a beautiful mountaintop.

2   7

"I've always wanted to see a real rain forest," said Barb. So they went to Brazil and saw thousands of trees and other plants along the Amazon River.

Next they went to Tanzania. They saw giraffes, elephants, and lions. "I didn't know that giraffes were so tall," said Barb.

4   5

Fold

Fold

COLORS ALL AROUND

Name _____

Fold

White is snow that covers the street.

3

Fold

✂

Blue is the sea where fish swim around,
Moving so smoothly without a sound.

8

✂

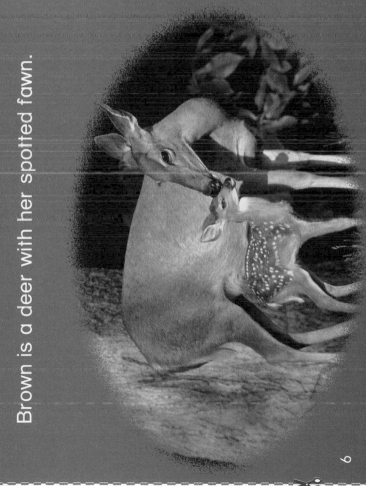

Brown is a deer with her spotted fawn.

6

✂

Directions: Help your child cut and fold the book. Read it together several times. Have your child find words with vowel digraphs **ea, oo, aw**, and vowel diphthongs **ow, ou, oi, ew**. Look for words with vowel pairs that make a long sound.

UNIT 6: Take-home Book

219

Red is a strawberry, juicy and sweet.

Green is a meadow moist with dew.

Fold

Fold

Orange is the pumpkin whose face I drew.

Yellow is the sun that we see at dawn.

5

2 7

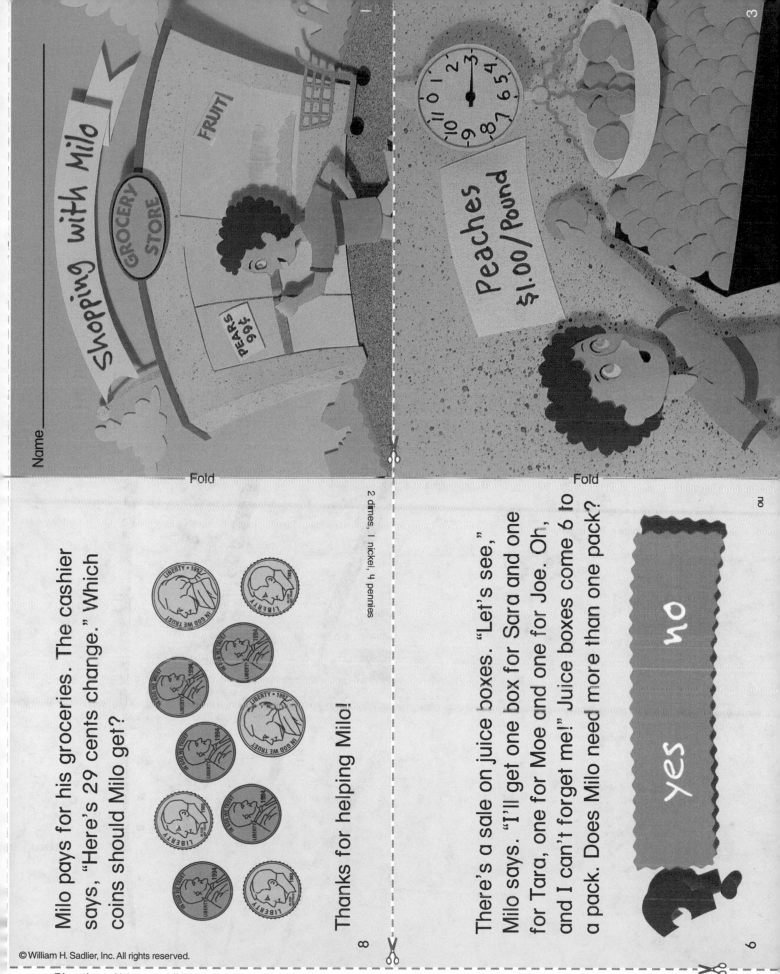

Name _____

Shopping with Milo

GROCERY STORE

FRUIT

PEARS 99¢

Peaches $1.00/Pound

Milo pays for his groceries. The cashier says, "Here's 29 cents change." Which coins should Milo get?

2 dimes, 1 nickel, 4 pennies

Thanks for helping Milo!

There's a sale on juice boxes. "Let's see," Milo says. "I'll get one box for Sara and one for Tara, one for Moe and one for Joe. Oh, and I can't forget me!" Juice boxes come 6 to a pack. Does Milo need more than one pack?

yes   no

Directions: Help your child cut and fold the book. Read it together several times.
Have your child find words that are contractions and words that end in **s, es,** and **ing**.

UNIT 7: Take-home Book

221

4

Milo thinks, "An apple a day keeps the doctor away. Maybe I'll eat an apple every day next week." How many apples should Milo buy for next week?

1 apple   7 apples   12 apples

7 apples

2

Let's help Milo with his shopping. Circle the best answer to each question.

Milo says, "I'll start with fruit." One pound of peaches costs $1.00. Milo gets 3 pounds. How much will he spend on peaches?

$1.00 $3.00 $8.00

$3.00

JUICES

1 OR 2?

APPLES

Name _____

A WONDERFUL DAY

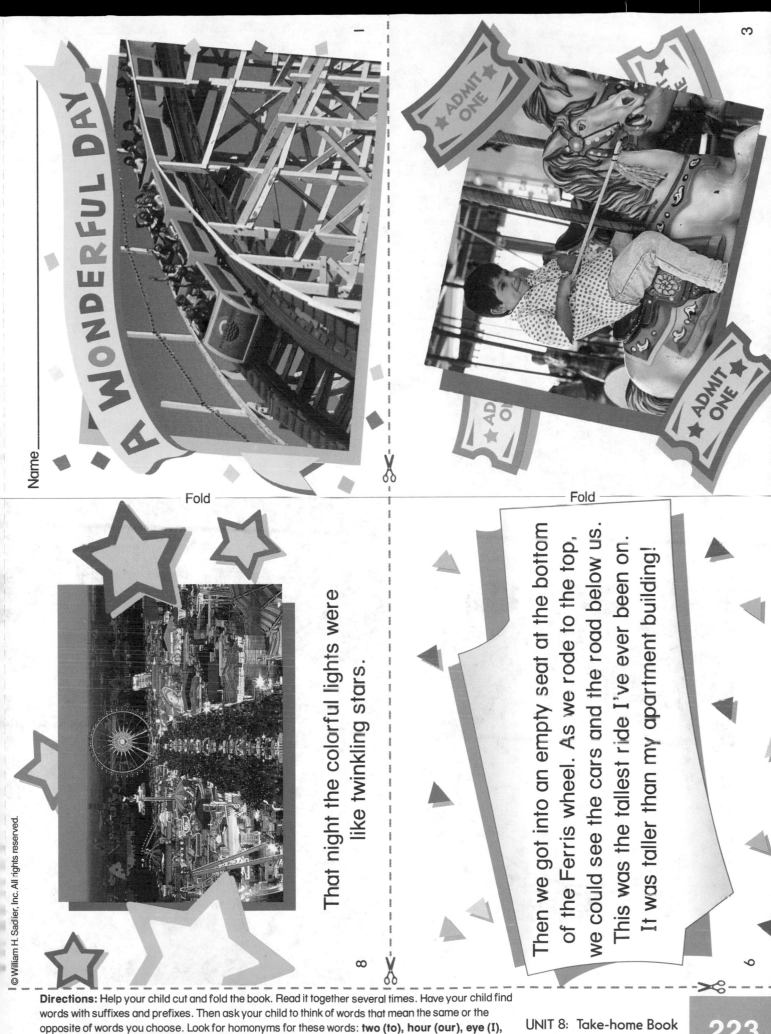

1

3

— Fold —

— Fold —

That night the colorful lights were like twinkling stars.

8

Then we got into an empty seat at the bottom of the Ferris wheel. As we rode to the top, we could see the cars and the road below us. This was the tallest ride I've ever been on. It was taller than my apartment building!

6

Directions: Help your child cut and fold the book. Read it together several times. Have your child find words with suffixes and prefixes. Then ask your child to think of words that mean the same or the opposite of words you choose. Look for homonyms for these words: **two (to), hour (our), eye (I), road (rode), knight (night).**

UNIT 8: Take-home Book

223

Next we rode on an unusual roller coaster. The cars went upside down around a huge loop. I was thankful when that ride ended!

Last summer my family went to the biggest amusement park I've ever seen. There were hundreds of families there.

First we went on the merry-go-round. The music played loudly as our horses moved up and down.

Fold

Fold